That endless, exhausting crusade for appro[...]
writer, Jennifer Dukes Lee takes you to th[...]
takes one stunning hammer to the foot of [...]
book—and walk free.

ANN VOSKAMP, Author of the *New York Times* bestseller *One Thousand Gifts*

Love Idol is a book that is going to set a lot of women free. It's a journey of grace, truth, and beautiful freedom. Jennifer Dukes Lee takes her readers by the hand and leads us to the home our hearts all long for deep inside—a place of true acceptance.

HOLLEY GERTH, Bestselling author of *You're Already Amazing*

Has Jennifer Dukes Lee been reading my journals? In all seriousness, *Love Idol* taps into something countless women struggle with. As I read Jennifer's tale of pursuing accolades and accomplishments instead of resting in God's absolute love for her, I was reminded of my own futile attempts to impress people—and God—with my achievements. I've been a fan of Jennifer for a long time, and I'm an even bigger one now. *Love Idol*'s gorgeously crafted, warm writing style and deeply honest stories invite readers into Jennifer's world, while simultaneously pointing them toward their heavenly Father. This is a book I'll keep close at hand and recommend to many, many women.

DENA DYER, Contributing editor, The High Calling; professional speaker; author of *Wounded Women of the Bible: Finding Hope When Life Hurts*

I am so excited about the book you hold in your hands! You are about to embark on a journey of soul healing and emotional freedom. I love how Jennifer poetically crafts each sentence; I love her transparent heart for us, her readers; and best of all, I love the way she communicates the love of our Savior. *Love Idol* invites you on a journey that will change you from the inside out. Jesus has set His heart on you, and you're worth everything to Him. Today is a brand-new day to believe it, receive it, and walk in that treasured freedom.

SUSIE LARSON, National radio host, speaker, and author of *Your Beautiful Purpose*

Jennifer Dukes Lee has written a book that every woman needs to read, a book that speaks counterculturally, a book that whispers to the heart of every mother, daughter, wife, and sister who longs to find approval. Through simple prose and personal anecdotes, Jennifer reassures us that we were born preapproved. We don't have to keep striving for love because we were designed and created by Love itself. It is with great joy and conviction that I endorse this timely and poignant work.

EMILY T. WIERENGA, Author of *Chasing Silhouettes* and *Mom in the Mirror*

I read *Love Idol* slowly because I didn't want it to end. When I turned the final page, I closed the book and hugged it to my heart. I don't think I've ever read a book quite like this one. It is elegantly written, beautifully spoken, bravely crafted, and tenderly shared. *Love Idol* is a sparkling love letter from the God who rejoices over each one of us— exactly as we are.

DEIDRA RIGGS, Managing editor, The High Calling

Jennifer Dukes Lee's book is beautiful and honest. As I read her stories, mesmerized, I realize that all too often I can spot my own heart in the stories and on the pages of *Love Idol*, recognizing how I've caved to the world's expectations and craved approval and significance, turning away from my first Love: Jesus, the only One whose approval truly matters. *Love Idol* reminds us to turn back to Him, where we find we're already approved.

ANN KROEKER, Author of *Not So Fast: Slow-Down Solutions for Frenzied Families*

There is no fluff in this book. It is solid, biblically based, and very readable. Within the pages of Jennifer's words flows a gentle persuasion that whispers to our souls: you *are* loved, you *are* approved, you *are* my beloved. It is a message of hope that, if taken to heart, could free you from the tiring job of trying to be perfect. This book will encourage you and help you exchange your love idols for performance-free living.

MARILYN HONTZ, Author of *Shame Lifter* and *Listening for God*

Jennifer's writing is so real, so honest, so vulnerable, so powerful. As Jennifer bares her heart, she challenges each one of us to examine our own, teaching us how to dethrone the Love Idol and experience the life-transforming love of Jesus for ourselves.

CHRISTIN DITCHFIELD, Internationally syndicated radio host; author of *What Women Should Know about Facing Fear*

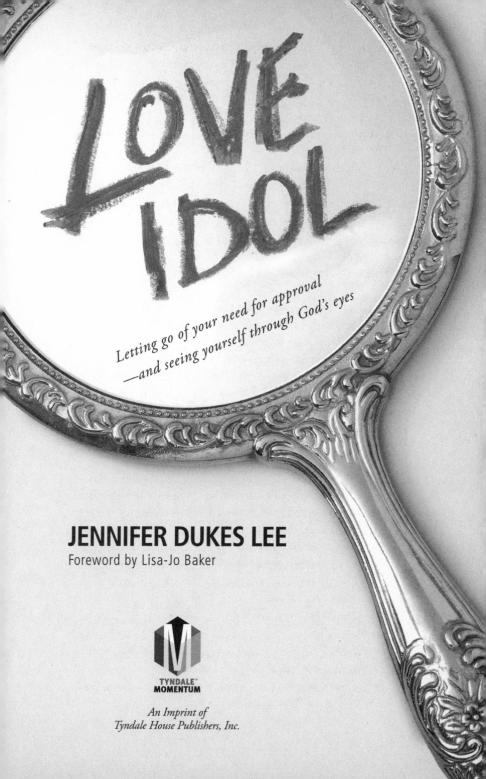

LOVE IDOL

Letting go of your need for approval
—and seeing yourself through God's eyes

JENNIFER DUKES LEE

Foreword by Lisa-Jo Baker

TYNDALE™
MOMENTUM

An Imprint of
Tyndale House Publishers, Inc.

Visit Tyndale online at www.tyndale.com.

Visit Tyndale Momentum online at www.tyndalemomentum.com.

Visit the author at jenniferdukeslee.com.

TYNDALE is a registered trademark of Tyndale House Publishers, Inc. *Tyndale Momentum* and the Tyndale Momentum logo are trademarks of Tyndale House Publishers, Inc. Tyndale Momentum is an imprint of Tyndale House Publishers, Inc.

Love Idol: Letting Go of Your Need for Approval—and Seeing Yourself through God's Eyes

Designed by Beth Sparkman

Published in association with William K. Jensen Literary Agency, 119 Bampton Court, Eugene, OR 97404.

Some of the names and identifying details of the women whose stories appear in this book have been changed to protect their privacy.

Library of Congress Cataloging-in-Publication Data

Lee, Jennifer Dukes.
    Love idol : letting go of your need for approval—and seeing yourself through God's eyes / Jennifer Dukes Lee.
        pages cm
    Includes bibliographical references.
    ISBN 978-1-4143-8073-5 (sc)
    1. Self-esteem—Religious aspects—Christianity. 2. God (Christianity)—Love. I. Title.
    BV4598.24.L44 2014
    248.4—dc23   2013036930

Printed in the United States of America

20	19	18	17	16	15	14
8	7	6	5	4	3	2

For Lydia and Anna:

May you always know the love that is already yours.

Contents

Foreword by Lisa-Jo Baker *ix*
Introduction: The *What* Idol? *xv*

CHAPTER 1   Picture Perfect *1*

CHAPTER 2   Clout *19*

CHAPTER 3   Conviction *31*

CHAPTER 4   Mud Pies *47*

CHAPTER 5   Bee Sting *59*

CHAPTER 6   "God's Got It" *73*

CHAPTER 7   "Do You Want to Get Well?" *93*

CHAPTER 8   Preapproved *111*

CHAPTER 9   Very Little *135*

CHAPTER 10   Cupped Hands *157*

CHAPTER 11   Bleachers *175*

CHAPTER 12   Haitian Hallelujah *193*

CHAPTER 13   Apelles *213*

Epilogue *231*
The Love Idol Movement *237*
Endnotes *239*
Discussion Guide *243*
Acknowledgments *255*
About the Author *259*

Foreword

It's FUNNY HOW you can grow up on the outside and still feel a little like thirteen on the inside. Or maybe a lot like thirteen on the inside. How you can have kids, a house, and a business card with your title right there at the top and still feel like a bit of a fraud.

If other people could only see how you couldn't fit comfortably into your jeans this morning or didn't know what to say as you sat at the lunch table across from two women far more accomplished and fashionably put together. Or how your five-year-old actually recited—in front of his entire class, the teacher, and God—an entire list of what you'd done to turn his Monday into a terrible, horrible, no-good, very bad day.

Then they'd know you couldn't possibly live up to the neatly lettered expectations printed loudly alongside your name, whether it's on a business card, the back of your journal, or the parent-teacher conference sign-up sheet.

So in the interest of full disclosure, I'll let you know that

Jennifer's e-mail asking me to write this foreword arrived on a day when I felt at perhaps my most scattered and ungreat. I typed these actual words back to her: "I'm sitting here such a mess this morning. Wet hair pulled back in a hair band and no makeup. It's that awful time of the month, and my house is a wreck. I feel dizzy and that there isn't enough sleep in the world to make up for the last seven years. I feel so empty and not enough."

Because the thing is, I often buy into the lie that there's something I can do, that I can manufacture, that I can claw my nails and my self-image into so I can drown out the panic and fear that plays the "you're not good enough" track on repeat in my head.

It's flat-out exhausting.

I know from firsthand experience. And I know from the hundreds of stories I've read at the blog I manage, www .incourage.me, a place where women the world over have bled their insecurities into the comment box during the last four years. Wonderful, accomplished, seemingly successful women have written the same words over and over again about feeling small and overlooked, about craving recognition and being afraid of failure.

Women I admire, women I love have crumbled when comparing themselves to their sisters and declared self-confidence bankruptcy. They've been tempted to check out of showing up again tomorrow.

Those women are not the exception.

So this book? This book has helped me get my bearings.

This book has logged many airline miles with me over the last month, jammed into my computer bag between my laptop and all those lists I'm behind on. This book has been a profound relief and a desperately needed, security-blanket reminder of who I am in Christ in a month that almost ate me alive with travel and insecurity.

And I've already given away the advance manuscript I was sent, because this book is like a life preserver I could pass along to a drowning friend.

Because we all so desperately want to know that who we are matters.

Like you and like Jennifer and like your friend who lives around the block or like the mom you met in the preschool pickup line, I want to know that the work I do and the kids I'm raising justify all this tiredness and make sense of my confused days. I want to believe that the laundry I just sorted or those pages of writing I just dredged out of my gut are going somewhere—that they're going to live larger than me in the lives of others.

I want to squeeze just one more round of affirmation out of my best friend, my editor, my mentor so that I can stew in the delicious assurance that I. Am. Worthy. I want to soak in that validation until my fingers turn pruny and my tired soul feels refreshed.

But tomorrow is waiting. And I know I'm going to wake up back at square one with the hair I've never figured out how to properly blow-dry and the boys who are being belligerent about breakfast as the school bus barrels toward our house. Then I'll be back to waiting for someone to come and tell me that I am something special.

We can waste a lot of days waiting.

We can waste a lot of time, beggars for praise.

We can waste away the DNA that makes our stories unique and necessary if we're constantly begging for praise handouts to prop them up.

But it's what we're used to. It's familiar. Comfortable. A pretty and reassuring reflection that we don't want to smash.

It's hard to get up and take up all that we are, all that we pretend to be, and all that Christ actually sees us as and walk forward in Him alone. It's hard and might require brand-new muscles, but I'm going for it.

So is Jennifer.

So can you.

All us daughters of the King can put one brave foot in front of the other. Because in the pages that follow, Jennifer offers a glimpse into how He truly sees us. Us with the messy hair and muffin tops that we try to hide behind stylish blouses, artfully draped just so. Us with the worry and insecurity, who work hard at fitting into groups and conferences and our own skin. Us who are all just wondering if we might find a new friend and tell her the story of our son who yelled and refused to get on the school bus and made us so embarrassed and so mad and so confused about being a grown-up.

Yes, all us sisters who need each other and a Savior who always sees the beauty within.

The beauty, affirmation, and love that is always there because it is always and only ever reflected in Him.

These pages are the reminder that you were already fully and deeply beloved before you were born and not because of anything you've done or haven't done. That there is a God who calls you by name right there in the midst of your deepest insecurity and holds out His hand, waiting for you to get up, pick up your story, and follow Him.

Lisa-Jo Baker

Mom to three very loud kids, social media manager to DaySpring, community manager for the millions of women who gather each year at www.incourage.me, and author of *Surprised by Motherhood: Everything I Never Expected about Being a Mom.*

The *What* Idol?

Hi, I'm Jennifer. I know, we've just met, but already a familiar anxiety is rising up inside my heart: I want you to like me.

For much of my life, I have lived like that. I have wanted people's approval. I have wanted to be a real somebody but have felt like a nobody. I'm not proud to say that I've been a people pleaser and a perfectionist and a prisoner to popular opinion. I hoped that others might *think* I had it all together, which was more important to me than actually having it all together.

Look at that, would you? See how I'm using the past tense, as if that woman were history? But here's the truth: Often, I still *am* that person.

Maybe you're like me, and you want to unchain yourself from your approval rating. You want to find deep contentment in who you are in Christ, not in what you do. You crave authentic joy in your life, based not on your gold-star performances, people's opinions of you, or the American dream with its temporary trappings, but on an identity secured for you through a loving Savior.

In short, you want to stop bowing down at the feet of the Love Idol.

I can almost hear your question. The . . . *what* idol? Love Idol? How can love be an idol? Love was God's idea. We were created in God's image, and God *is* love!

Paul wrote to the Corinthians: "These three remain: faith, hope and love. And the greatest of these is love."[1] Yet we take God's "greatest" and contort it into an idol. We twist our desire for approval into a false god.

Instead of resting in the love and approval of an unseen God, we chase after the temporary pleasures of human validation.

Whatever rules our hearts becomes our lord. The person who seeks approval and acceptance can become controlled by it. The person who is motivated primarily by a need for human affirmation is, in the end, ruled by it.

If we don't get the love and acceptance we crave, we're deflated. But if we do get the approval we want, we might not be any better off, for we are tricked into thinking our idols offer fulfillment.

And we keep going back for more.

This book is for any of us who want to live content in God's perfect love, freed up from the wearying demands of the Love Idol.

This is not a book of how-tos or tacked-on require-ments for the Christian life. It will not tell you what you must do to earn or gain more love and approval from others. Most of us have already tried that approach, and it hasn't worked. Rather, this is a book that woos you to open your hands to receive a love that is already yours. Together, we can wave the white flag, surrendering our need for human approval in exchange for a godly approval that is already bought and paid for. These words are for you and also for me, co-pilgrims on this journey of discovery. Wrapped in these pages are my heart's cry and my personal fight for freedom, offered to you. I pray that, together, we can give up on

- the inner critic who bruises, the mirror that accuses, and the mental playback that oozes with bad history;
- our knee-jerk response to try to please people;
- the idea that it's somehow all up to you and me, or that our reputations hinge on our own spotless performance;
- our penchant for self-criticism;
- our fear of trying because we're afraid we'll fail when people are watching;
- our inability to fully experience the love of God because we're waiting for proof from a spouse or a friend that we are worthy of his or her love;
- our longing to feel important;
- our appetite for being "known";
- our un-gospel notions about pleasing God.

Are you with me?

I hope so, because I need a friend on this journey.

Perhaps you're like me—in need of a fresh reminder that we're *already* loved by the One who made us. These words are for those of us who know what the Bible says—that our identity is found in Jesus—but who continue to find ourselves snared in a sprint for significance among inhabitants of planet Earth.

Some of you hold these words in your hands because you grew up believing that love and approval are earned assets—but that no one ever cared to invest in you. You grew up being told you were unlovable. You were neglected or abused by someone who disregarded the treasure that you are. Perhaps you struggle to know what love really is, because someone you should have been able to trust perverted it.

Your problem, perhaps, is this: you feel you've had to work your way toward love. You had an overbearing father or a mother who demonstrated her approval only when you performed according to her standards. Or maybe your church left you with the impression that you had to earn grace and thus love.

On the other hand, perhaps you grew up in a home like mine—where you experienced love and security. When you went to bed, your dad pulled the sheet tight under your chin and kissed you on the cheek before he turned out the light. All these years later, if you were to stretch out on the psychiatrist's couch, he'd be hard-pressed to find something deep in your past that triggered your need for approval.

I don't have a good excuse for how messed up I've been, as you'll see in the pages ahead, other than the fact that I am part of the human race, which has a history of turning God's greatest gifts into idols.

That's right—not all idols are made of gold. Some of the most dangerous idols are cleverly disguised in the clothing of God's gifts—food, sex, pleasure, and even love.

And they leave us lovesick.

Friend, where have you twisted love into a false god? Where have you gone looking for love, approval, and respect?

Our culture bombards us with the message that if we meet certain standards, life will be better. We are told that the answers to our deepest aches can be discovered if we work harder, climb faster, get prettier—all of it apart from God.

Maybe you looked for validation in the backseat of a car, at the table with the important people, or on the last empty barstool of the tavern. Maybe you've looked for approval from a distant spouse, a son who won't come home, a coworker who dismisses your innovative ideas, or a father who still thinks you'll never be good enough. Your quest for approval has left you completely empty. You want to be seen, to be known. But you feel like an invisible "nobody."

Or maybe it's all looked rather harmless. In fact, on paper, your quest for love and approval might look like it actually *worked*. After all, you might have landed at the top of the honor roll, on the Homecoming Court, on the Chamber of Commerce board, on everybody's Christmas card list, or in the glass office with upholstered chairs.

The big star in the spotlight has felt it; the "nobody" with her back against the wall has craved it: the sweet taste of validation and approval.

Satan loves to whisper this one question into every human ear: "What will people think of you?" In a cold sweat, we respond to that question by throwing our money, energy, and time into what we think will give us joy, applause, acceptance, and a little bit more respect.

But no matter how much we get—or how good we are—there's always someone doing life better, writing her story more poetically, speaking her words more eloquently, living her days more gracefully, raising her children more patiently, being promoted more regularly. (And she probably has better hair.)

I know, because I've found myself in the cultural rat race. I've scurried up corporate ladders, only to find the rungs never reach high enough to satisfy. For years, I worked sixty-hour weeks at newspapers, hoping to garner the respect of editors and peers with front-page stories and scoops. I've been a social chameleon, shifting to fit in with the crowd. I've tried to do everything perfectly and make others happy—all because I wanted more love. And I've employed various techniques—fake smiles and witty Facebook statuses among them—to make you *think* I'm okay when on the inside I'm breaking.

So what is the chief end of all my striving? Has it brought me lasting joy?

In some ways, I've been a raging success, at least according to cultural barometers. But you cannot measure the health of a woman's soul by yardsticks, scales, or approval ratings. Hear me now. I'm evidence that a person can get her fill and never feel more empty.

But I've also felt like the nobody. Maybe you can relate. Maybe you've never been asked to the cool kids' table. You look at your Facebook news feed and realize suddenly: you're the only one who didn't get invited.

Or maybe you're a pastor with a half-empty church, a writer who can't get a publisher to take one look at your manuscript, a volunteer whose contributions are overlooked every single time.

You think you wow no one in your life.

In the midst of it, you can feel like a complete loser.

But take heart: There is greatest hope for the biggest losers. People who lose their lives for the sake of Christ end up winning, living the life for which they were created (see Matthew 10:39).

When I began the process of writing this book, I enlisted a prayer team of friends that included a pastor. He agreed to pray, even before he knew the content of the book.

He texted me later with a question: "What is the book about?"

I texted a response, with these words exactly: "It is a book about making peace with yourself and with whom God made you to be. It is for people who crave approval . . . and who fear that at any moment the world will see what a mess they really are. Funny, because you might think a person should be cured before they write such a book, but even as I write, I find myself in the midst of this battle daily."

One minute later, my phone beeped with the pastor's texted response: "That is the thing—the cure is the process."

The cure *is* the process.

So begins the journey. You and I step onto the path together, arm in arm, daring one another to find our truest selves along this winding road, homeward bound. My own life is a case study of the way that the human need for love manifests itself in a variety of ways: from approval seeking to chasing the good life. First I pull back the curtain on my own past—a narrative rife with mistakes. Then I invite you to journey with me into a present-day discovery, exploring the immeasurable ways that you and I are already loved scandalously by God, who gave us His only begotten Son.

I do not write this as the master. I write instead as a fellow traveler, stumbling her way along, awed over the most stunning love story ever told. And trust me, you have a starring role.

One of His beloved,

Jennifer

Love Idol *includes a four-week*
discussion guide that begins on page 243.

CHAPTER I

PICTURE PERFECT

Define yourself radically as one beloved by God. This is
the true self. Every other identity is illusion.

BRENNAN MANNING

THE STORY OF this approval-craving people pleaser begins
in the front row of a sixth-grade classroom.

I'm the scrawny girl holding her breath, overinflated
with air and anxiety. I clench a No. 2 pencil in my sweaty
little fist, as if I might muster up superhuman strength to
squeeze the lead straight out of it. The language arts
teacher click-clacks her high heels on the linoleum floor,
delivering graded papers to a room full of children who—
with the exception of me—slump with carefree ease at their
desks. I wonder if they have been lulled into some kind of
post-lunch trance, induced by the cafeteria's chipped beef
and potatoes. Do they not realize that Mrs. Huseman is

distributing grades for *the biggest project of our entire lives* . . . or at least of the sixth grade?

With glacial speed, the teacher slides graded papers face-down onto the wood-veneer tops of our desks. Vaughan's paper airplane zooms past Shane's head, bounces off the chalkboard, and then crash-lands on the teacher's desk. The boys snicker, Mrs. Huseman scolds, and I retreat into a private tsunami of worry. Who has time for child's play at a moment like this? My arms stiffen with fear, paralyzed by the overachiever's coup de grâce: the prospect of getting a B on my project.

At last, the teacher pauses beside me. She presses my grade onto the desk and pats my back, an attempt to offer reassurance for an overwrought child who does not want to disappoint her teacher or her parents. I flip the paper over and hold my breath until my darting eyes find what I crave.

And I do. I find an A+ inked in a corner. Only then do I exhale, in one long, warm stream of air. The thin, red lines of a single vowel coax my fears into remission. This fulfills my daily requirement of approval, and now I can breathe. At least until tomorrow.

I don't know what I would have done if I had gotten a B. I was never brave enough to try such a daring thing as *that*.

My whole life, I have lived this way, in a breathless scamper for significance and the approval that comes with it. I have performed, climbed, raced, jockeyed, and postured for it.

I've feared rejection. I've wanted to be a lot of things: prettier, skinnier, smarter, better. In all the striving, the graffiti of human praise defaced real love.

I have wanted the A—not just on my sixth-grade paper but in life.

You can call it perfectionism if you want. But that's just a symptom of the bigger problem. I've wanted to be approved. I've wanted to be loved.

I've forgotten that I already am.

The Love Idol has enslaved me, chaining me to my approval rating. I have been addicted to being liked.

And the world is a buffet, dishing out heaping portions of flimsy praise: crowns for the homecoming queens, trophies for the first-place finishers, glossy covers for the world's most beautiful. We fill our plates, feeding on lies about love. We nibble crumbs of approval and always leave the table hungry for more. We measure love and respect by numbers: Facebook friends, checkbook balances, monthly sales quotas, and dress sizes.

It never fills.

We start young, looking for love somewhere outside Eden before we're even able to tie our shoes or count to ten. We enter the world wrinkled and flailing as if we already fear abandonment. Someone cuts the cord and puts a striped beanie on us, as we cry out to be held. And so begins a lifelong quest for love.

Enter Satan.

The world's oldest liar gets us to forget that we were

God's idea in the first place. We don't always remember that there is a very real God on a very real throne who calls us His beloved. The slithering enemy convinces us that our Maker's love is never enough, never was. And Satan continually asks us to consider what others are thinking of us. He tries to make us forget about God. Martin Luther calls it sin: "The sin underneath all our sins is to trust the lie of the serpent that we cannot trust the love and grace of Christ and must take matters into our own hands."

With our distrusting eyes off our Maker, we really do take matters into our own hands, like modern-day Eves grabbing for the polished fruit of cultural standards and expectations.

We cannot rationally explain the enormity of God's love or why Christ would die for us "while we were still sinners" (Romans 5:8). So we live like we don't believe it at all.

I have lived like I don't believe it at all.

I've doubted His love. I've distrusted His covenant.

It's April 2, 1972—the day after April Fools' Day— and the Rev. Vickery holds me in the crook of his arm. He sprinkles water on my forehead at the front of the United Methodist Church, then hoists my curled body higher, an infant queen, shrieking. The congregants in the creaky wooden pews applaud.

At age three, I toddle toward the altar in patent leather shoes, standing on that same square foot of red carpet where I was baptized. And now, I've come to sing "Jesus Loves Me" with the cherub choir.

Years later, I kneel there to receive my first Communion.

At age thirteen, I wear a white robe and confirm my baptismal vows. And then, one Christmas Eve, I sit in a folding chair on that very spot, playing the part of Mary, mother of God, cradling her Fisher-Price Savior.

But I remain the April fool, believing lies about what love really means. I confess now that I have not fully believed the promise of my baptism. If I'm gut-level honest, I've lived like an agnostic. Me, a woman girded by Christ's teachings from age three. Me, a woman who serves Communion, volunteers at vacation Bible school, selects worship music for her congregation. In the sanctuary, I sing of His great love with tears rolling down my cheeks. Yet in my everyday life, I have at times treated those songs like mouthed abstractions. Although it has not been intentional, the old nature rises up against my new self. It pains me to write these words, but it's true: At times, my divided heart has looked for significance everywhere else but the altar. The world is a cacophony of distraction and man-made applause, drowning out the sound of Christ calling.

I cannot pinpoint a trigger in my personal history to explain why I have sought human approval like I have over these years. Yes, my parents valued and rewarded hard work. They expected me to give my best effort in school. But I never felt that I had to earn their love and approval. I knew I was loved because I was theirs. Period.

It is, perhaps, the way I am wired, no different from being born with hazel eyes. And it is, in a sense, the way we're *all* wired. God created within us this need to love and to be loved, a beautiful inner longing that is designed to drive us toward Him. But our old nature can twist our hunger for love, so we begin to crave the approval of people over the approval of God.

God's Word suggests that this is part of the human condition. Scripture addresses it repeatedly, warning us against the temptation to choose the temporal. In fact, the warning became a theme for Paul throughout his letters. He wrote, "Our purpose is to please God, not people" (1 Thessalonians 2:4).

But the truth is, we don't always want to please God. We actually *like* pleasing people, because it feels good. The sound of applause reminds us not only that we're doing a good job but, equally important, that we're not messing up in front of a live audience. Since we can't hear God's "attagirl" in our human ears, the crowd's applause lets us know that we matter in the world.

Soon, even the applause isn't enough. We secretly hope the audience will give us a standing ovation, so we keep singing and dancing. We live for the perpetual encore.

What an exhausting life.

My friend Shari knows how exhausting that life can be. She says her need for approval has caused her to question her worth in almost every area of life: as a wife, a mom, a friend, an employee, a Christian. But the question she has struggled with the longest is this: Am I a good daughter?

"I love my parents deeply. I have had a good relationship with them most of my life," Shari says. "Yet there was one thing that I really wanted to hear from them, one thing that I sought hard after for many, many years. I wanted to hear them say, 'I am so proud of you.'"

For years, Shari heard her parents boast about the accomplishments of one of her siblings. "Each time I did something, I waited for the approval that I hoped would come . . . it never did. And I was left disappointed and sad," she recalls.

Shari says her need for approval became an addiction, like she was a drug addict craving another hit. When she couldn't get it from her parents, she looked for it in other relationships. "Eventually that next 'hit' can't come soon enough, and it isn't enough. You need more and more to satisfy," she says.

Like Shari, I grew to desire "the next hit." As a child, I loved compliments because they let me know I mattered. Criticism could downright deflate my whole spirit.

Early in life, my two older sisters and younger brother dubbed me the Golden Child. The name was, perhaps, a well-meaning joke for the straight-A sister with the smoothed-down bangs and color-coordinated closet. I wore the nickname like a badge. It felt like real praise.

And just behind the praise, I could hear the mocking, high-pitched giggles of my neuroses. These were the voices in my head, and they looked like two snobbish Valley Girls, making themselves at home in my teenage brain. *Golden*

Child? Like, whatever! That's what they would say, with an eye roll. In my mind, those two girls wore stirrup pants and neon hair scrunchies. They sashayed around the middle of my cerebrum like they owned the place.

My parents went out of their way to make sure that I knew I would still be loved, even if I failed miserably. One morning comes back now with startling clarity: the morning of a junior high track meet in 1985. I told Dad I was weary of the embarrassment of last-place finishes. I wanted to quit. I folded my arms on the kitchen table and dropped my head down, sobbing. Dad put a hand on my shoulder and urged me to simply try my hardest, focusing on something he called my "personal best." That rainy afternoon, I ran twice around an asphalt oval in northwest Iowa. I came across the finish line dead last in the 800-meter race. I didn't know it yet, but I had improved my personal best by several seconds. Lungs burning and chest heaving, I put my hands on my hips and looked up into the bleachers. Through the drizzle, I saw Mom and Dad, both of them on their feet, with their hands high in the air, applauding.

They loved and approved of me, in spite of my lack-luster finish.

Yet I much preferred bringing home As on my projects and high ratings from musical contests. Sure, my parents cheered when I lost, but somewhere on the inside of me, I would rather have had them be proud of a winner, not a last-place finisher.

Even if my parents didn't criticize me, those snobbish

Valley Girls did. They were belligerent opportunists, reminding me where I failed. That's the job of inner critics: to stick a foot in the door of your brain and remind you what a loser you are, never mind what your God says about you.

In my teenage journal—a spiral-bound Mead notebook—I often wrote about the pain those two inner critics inflicted on my tender soul. Last year, I found that yellow notebook hidden underneath the mattress of my childhood bed. I remember experiencing a sinking sense of disappointment when, as an adult, I flipped through pages to find that not a whole lot had changed since childhood. I could practically hear the Valley Girls—now grown-up women wearing Prada—snickering while I reread old words:

"Why do I feel this way?" I wrote at age sixteen. "If there were 100 people I knew and 99 of them liked me, I'd very likely concentrate on the one that disliked me because I want *everyone* to like me." Even then, my downcast soul tried to remind myself of the truth. I wrote at the bottom of the page these words: "God is love! I am loved."

True enough, I had written it on college-ruled paper, that I was loved by a Savior. Yet I lived another way, and it would be years before I would recognize this as a spiritual problem that needed fixing.

Approval intoxicated me. By the time I was a teenager, I was learning how to fill my addiction: with bylines. I was only sixteen years old when I felt the thrill of seeing my name in print. I had begun writing stories for our local weekly paper as part of our school's career-exploration program. They were small stories about Easter egg hunts and town baseball matchups. But I was *writing*. Publicly. For a real-life audience. People would tell me they liked the way I could tell a story.

As a senior in high school, I made a campus visit to Iowa State University. A journalism-school recruiter gave me a tour of the college's newspaper office. I noticed right away the glass office in the corner and made a vow to myself that I would run that place someday.

Three years later, at age twenty-one, the *Iowa State Daily*'s masthead listed my name as editor. I loved chasing the story, experiencing the thrill of front-page bylines. It made me feel powerful, approved, and respected. Every summer, instead of going home to relax for a couple of months, I worked at newspapers. In the summer of 1994, I drove my Geo Storm halfway across the country after landing a highly regarded internship at the *Sacramento Bee*.

I think it's important for you to know that I value hard work and excellence, the kind that will have a college student aiming high in his or her career. Eagerness and ambition, rightly channeled in our workplaces and homes, make the world a better place for all of us. My trouble, of course, came because I worshiped what my work could give me, instead of what God already had waiting for me.

But my accomplishments never once satisfied me long-term, no matter how many "attagirls" I got.

I suppose a part of me knew that the answer rested in Jesus. I would pay Him an occasional visit by darkening the doorway of a church now and then. But mostly I saw God as a disinterested third party—or worse, the fairy-tale hero of nicely packaged Sunday school stories. "God's love" was an assurance that I left in my yellow notebook, a holy promise that I slipped in a box under the bed of my childhood home. It was a promise that I had forgotten. I was becoming fluent, not in God's love but in status and achievement.

The world is full of rankings and résumé lines that make you forget about God, report cards that let you know whether you made the grade in this great big world.

Any of us can look back on our childhood lives and remember the lists that shaped us: honor rolls published in the local paper, school-play casting calls, homecoming courts, birthday party invitations, and more. When we grow up, the lists grow up with us: the Fortune 500, the 50 Most Beautiful People in the World, the Top 100 Bloggers, the richest, the sexiest, the most relevant. Even Christian leaders have come up with online lists to tell us which authors are the most influential.

In a world of list makers, how can we begin to live only for the Maker's list? In a world that says, "Climb higher to be noticed," how can we bow lower?

One of my dearest friends, Trish—a self-described approval addict—knows about the lists, the ones that let you know you're valued. She likes how it feels to be picked.

Trish says her approval addiction can manifest itself in

the ugliest ways right in our own church. She likes knowing that people can count on her—to sing a solo, sew
Christmas-pageant costumes, decorate the altar, and lead
a mission project.

"I can channel my inner Sally Fields at church," she
says. "You know, 'They like me; they really like me!'"

At times, she says, her need for an "attagirl" from the
pews can morph into an ugly monster called pride.

"There are no acronyms like AA to help us," she says.
"There are no well-known support groups, no twelve-step
programs for our problem. Most people wouldn't classify
it as a problem, let alone an addiction. I mean, everyone
likes to be appreciated. If only that were the extent of it."

Trish and I half-joke that we ought to start up a flagship
AAA—Approval Addicts Anonymous.

She and I confess to each other about times when we
have preferred the approval of people over the approval of
God, even in our church. Our old nature hovers, threaten-
ing to bring us down daily, to make us want to be noticed.

Shari, Trish, and I have to fight this war again and again,
because the enemy hasn't surrendered. He knows he can't
have us for eternity, so he wants as much of us as he can have
while the earth spins under our feet. He'll follow us straight
through the glass doors of our churches if he has to.

But we have decided that it's a battle worth fighting. We
really do want liberation from the Love Idol.

We ache to live our Christ identity more fully, instead of
living a life yielded to our approval ratings. Life in Christ is

not a popularity contest. It is not a materialistic chase for medals, money, or Twitter @mentions.

But how can we really begin to uproot the Love Idol? How do we begin to understand that God's love is the only love that slakes our thirst for approval? How can we shed the self-obsessed culture in which we live?

I want to live the right answers to those questions.

I want to live like I'm loved.

Because I am.

～ℒ～

Mrs. Huseman, my sixth-grade teacher, knew the problem, at least in part. She named it for me, but I didn't know that day what she meant. And at first, I took it as a compliment.

Mrs. Huseman wrote the word in loopy cursive: "perfectionist."

Naturally, I saw the A+ before I saw the P-word. But when I discovered that word—*perfectionist*—I locked my gaze upon it as if it possessed a certain magic. I read her note while twirling strands of hair around my index finger.

"You have a perfectionist quality in you that I so often see as a great asset," Mrs. Huseman wrote.

I blushed.

There was more. She filled two sides of that pink notepaper: "Beware of it, however, and try to always view things with an open mind. After all, there always will be tomorrow."

Her words were a well-intentioned warning for a girl who yearned to be the best at something. *Anything.* I wanted to

know that I was loved and valued not just by my parents—
which I was—but by the masses in Marathon, Iowa (population 352). I wanted the pat on the back, the neon-light
validation from my teachers and peers, and perhaps a one-
paragraph announcement in the community-church bulletin
informing the public. I wanted to feel significant. I realize all
of that now.

If I could, I would sit knee-to-knee with my twelve-
year-old self on the school playground, take her by the
hand, and persuade her to cut herself some slack. I'd tell
her she ought to heed the words of her wise and discerning
language arts teacher. I'd show her how to make a paper
airplane. I'd tell her to go ahead and wear her favorite
fuchsia-colored leg warmers, even if the other girls made
fun of her. I'd mess up her hair.

I'd dare her to get a B.

But back then, I didn't hear the teacher's warning. I doubt
I would have listened to my older, wiser self either. I heard
only that one single word, and I let it roll around in my
mouth: *perfectionist.* I rather liked how it sounded. Because
if you took off the last six letters, you were left with something . . . perfect.

I knew what perfect meant. Perfect meant approval.
Perfect meant significant. Perfect meant contentment.

But, fat chance of *perfect.* On the ball field and in the
mirror, I was the antonym of perfection. I figured that if I
was God's idea, He must have been taking a vacation when
His helpers pieced me together on the assembly line.

When I looked at my reflection, I saw an odd-looking little creature staring back with crooked teeth. I wore a bra, not because I needed one, but because I wanted to fit in with the crowd—which held considerable sway over almost every decision I made. I wanted good grades to please my parents, who valued hard work and straight As. I made up silly lyrics to songs, hoping to win my friends' approval. And I stole a necklace from the jewelry store to impress the popular girl who dared me to do it.

I knew what the Bible said about me, but I measured my worth by other barometers—the mirror, report cards, and my performance among peers—even if it broke well-established moral rules.

On the playground, I was voted as the kid most likely to trip over her shoelaces. When team captains chose sides for kickball, I was the last one picked. My top dresser drawer held a collection of green and yellow ribbons—the consolation prizes for runners who slogged across the finish line last. I did score two points in basketball in the seventh grade. Trouble was, I scored for the rival team.

No, I wasn't perfect at all. But I wouldn't mind if Mrs. Huseman *thought* I was.

Mrs. Huseman had instructed us to write our autobiographies for a class project.

Mine included the high points, naturally: crisp certificates from piano contests, photographs of me posing for the local newspaper with a shiny French horn propped on my lap. I strategically left out the green and yellow ribbons, or the fact that I lost the district spelling bee the year before on a three-letter word.

My autobiography also included a detailed, handwritten plan for the next ninety-three years of life. I set high expectations and mapped out a future that would, I hoped, give me the sense of validation that I deeply craved. At age twelve, I was an early adopter of the now-popular school of thought that if one wants to achieve her dreams, she should write them down. I was my own life coach. While most girls my age planned slumber parties, I mapped life strategies. I wrote that I would marry a handsome man and birth twins—one girl and one boy—all while managing dual careers as a highly acclaimed psychiatrist and a famous book author. Death would not come knocking until age 105.

What I didn't know then is that life has a way of making its own plans, no matter what you write down.

But in that single moment, my planning paid off handsomely. I got an A+ on my autobiography. Along with the grade, Mrs. Huseman wrote me that two-sided note. "You really are a busy girl," she wrote. "And your future—well— you certainly have it all spec'd out! If you do live to be 105, you'll have many tomorrows!"

I read and reread her letter that day in the classroom.

Perfect? Isn't that what Mrs. Huseman said I was?

If I couldn't be the fastest runner or the prettiest girl, maybe I could be perfect at *trying* to be perfect. That had to be good, right?

I squeezed my eyes tight and could almost hear the

crowd's applause—the roar of validation ringing in my ears. I envisioned my name tacked to the bulletin board in the school lobby. The announcer's voice crackled over the gymnasium's loudspeaker—*Here she is, Miss Jennifer D-U-UUUUKES!* And not a single soul in those bleachers would remember that I was the goofy-looking klutz who once scored a layup for the wrong team.

I filed Mrs. Huseman's letter away at the bottom of a dresser drawer, back in a decade when banana combs were still *en vogue*. I didn't read it again for another quarter of a century. I was too busy making all those dreams come true, gathering up a couple of decades worth of "attagirls." It would be years before I learned that a woman can scoop up almost everything her little heart desires, while missing out entirely on what her emaciated soul really needs.

I was firmly in the grip of the Love Idol.

Whose "attagirl" do you value most? (Find additional questions for reflection in the discussion guide at the back of the book.)

CHAPTER 2

CLOUT

While the goal of the American dream is to make much of us,
the goal of the gospel is to make much of God.

DAVID PLATT

YOU DON'T ALWAYS know where the Love Idol has been
lurking in your past until you rewind the tapes and watch
your life on the playback. And then, years later, you see the
shadow of that wretched idol right there when you flip
through the photo album of your life.

You might see this:

- Your painfully crooked teeth in your third-grade
  school picture, a reminder of how much you wanted
  to look like one of the popular girls
- Your high school prom photo, which brings back
  a strange sadness as you remember how you got
  dumped the following week

- The photograph of you with your smiling spouse and children, the last family portrait taken before your husband walked out on you for someone else
- That picture of you mugging in your cubicle, a reminder of how the boss canned you when you didn't meet sales expectations

Each of those moments represents a weak spot, an opening for the Love Idol to sneak into your life and trick you into looking away from God for something you crave: approval, respect, a pat on the back, or a sense that you belong.

Me? I flip the photo-album pages to find a professional head shot from my days as a news reporter. In the picture, I'm wearing a navy-blue suit and a half smile that projects a false confidence.

I didn't see the Love Idol's shiny hands around my throat back then, but I see them clearly now. By that time, I was living my childhood dreams, and the Love Idol already had me locked in its vise. My life looked an awful lot like the American definition of success.

I fidgeted with the brassy buttons lining the front of my navy-blue suit jacket, rolling each one between my white-tipped, manicured nails. I adjusted my skirt and checked my beige nylons for snags.

I quadruple-checked the contents of my briefcase. All of

it was, predictably, still there: my tape recorder, four pens, extra batteries, two reporter notebooks, a list of questions. My interview subject and I would have fifteen minutes together, at most. But a reporter can never be too prepared when she is about to meet a real "somebody."

As Mrs. Huseman had said years earlier, I had it "all spec'd out"—not just my briefcase, but my very life. Years of hard work had led to this moment; at least that's the way it felt when I looked out the lobby windows. A long streak of black glided past the front doors. The limousine had arrived.

"Mrs. Lee?" A squarish man walked toward me, wearing a striped tie. He motioned for me to follow him.

I followed the suited fellow out through the revolving glass door. An expressionless man with dark sunglasses and an earphone stood next to the limousine. The afternoon sun glinted off the chrome handle of the passenger-side door, which someone had unlatched. The man held out a hand, with the palm up—a gesture to invite me into the dim, muffled chamber.

I ducked my head in and, with as much poise as I could, uttered five words:

"Good afternoon, Mr. Vice President."

I slid inside, sinking deep into a leather seat next to the day's priority news assignment: Al Gore. Cool air shot through the vents. The door shut behind me, sealing me inside a fancy car with my well-stocked briefcase, a host of personal insecurities, and a man who wanted to be the leader of the free world.

"Good afternoon, Mrs. Lee." He extended a hand. We shook briefly.

The vice president ran a hand through his hair and propped a foot on the limousine seat in front of him. He let out his breath in a long sigh and then looked right at me, smiling, with a disarming charisma that didn't match the stiff, dry personality I had anticipated. He slapped his hands on his thighs and asked the first question: "So. What do you want to talk about?"

I stammered, then flipped open my notebook, hoping that a small-town Iowa girl posing as a big-shot reporter could find a crumb of confidence somewhere between the thin lines of a Steno pad.

The Love Idol's captives at once crave and dread these high-pressure opportunities. We want the important assignment, but we live in fear of blowing it. Our inner critics start yammering before we even say a word.

In the grip of the Love Idol, we are also habitually sorry for everything.

Hours earlier I had stood with slumped shoulders in the newsroom, apologizing to my editor. I begged his forgiveness for not landing my story on page one in the morning paper. And I was sorry that I hadn't yet talked to the state legislator from Carroll County who had called. And I was sorry for not trying harder to get the governor's spokesman on the phone. And I was sorry for . . .

"Jennifer," my editor had interrupted me, then leaned back in his chair, shaking his head and laughing. "Are you super religious? Because you've seriously got the most severe case of guilt I have ever seen."

I was not, in fact, super religious, nor had it occurred to me that I was suffering from guilt. I did, however, promptly apologize for being so sorry all the time. And then I walked back to my cubicle.

Fear seemed a more accurate word than *guilt.* The Love Idol's prey live in fear of failing to meet expectations. We fear the facade will drop and our peers or coworkers will discover the flawed us, the perpetually freaked-out us. We cringe over the threat of disapproval, real or imagined. And we feel as if we continually need to explain away any potential flaw.

My life had become a defensive posture against possible criticism.

Rather than enjoying the incredible opportunities that life in journalism had afforded me—moments like interviewing the vice president of the United States—I got myself all wigged-out.

That afternoon with Vice President Gore, I launched into my questions, furrowing my brow, narrowing my eyes a bit, and tilting my head just so. I had practiced that look in the mirror, hoping it would make me seem more reporter-like— or at least a bit older than twenty-nine. Mr. Gore was a candidate for the 2000 presidential election, and one in a long line of candidates whom I had interviewed over the past year. I was a political reporter for the *Des Moines Register*, which dubbed itself "The Newspaper Iowa Depends Upon." Since

1972, the year I was born, Iowa has held the distinction of hosting the nation's first caucus, an important barometer in determining the electability of a presidential candidate. Every four years, the Des Moines International Airport becomes a revolving airstrip for people who want to make 1600 Pennsylvania Avenue their home address. And in 2000, all of them returned my phone calls. I ate bruschetta with Alan Keyes. I repeatedly called Senator John Edwards to ask if he would run in the future. George W. Bush made time for my questions.

The dictionary has a word for that sort of thing: *clout.*

And isn't that what I'd longed for? Didn't I write it down, clear back in the sixth grade with Mrs. Huseman? I had vowed to be an author, sure. But wasn't this close— this moment, right here, with a pen and a notebook in my hands? This is what I'd worked hard for. This is what I'd schooled and studied and interned for. Wasn't my life's purpose found somewhere next to the important people? Maybe this was what people meant when they talked about a calling. I had dreamed about it and then opened my eyes to find myself living it: riding in limos, asking the tough questions, breaking the stories, walking onstage to accept the occasional award, getting the plush assignments, earning the pay raises.

I had my own religion, and I was worshiping at the altar of the American dream, having been baptized by bylines.

James Truslow Adams coined that phrase, "American dream," in 1931. He defined it as "a dream of social order in which each man and each woman shall be able to attain to the fullest stature of which they are innately capable, *and be recognized by others for what they are*, regardless of the fortuitous circumstances of birth or position" (emphasis mine).[1]

Haven't you and I wanted some of that? Haven't we pined for a little validation? We have wanted to be—as Adams wrote—"recognized."

Somewhere inside our unsure little selves, we yearn to know that we matter in the world. We want to know that our lives have value, though we may have false notions about how such value should be measured. We *do* crave a love that we can feel—something like a pat on the back.

As a child, I suppose I had learned differently from people like Hortense Cochrane, my Sunday school teacher. I suppose I had learned that Jesus' love was grander than anything I could ever imagine. When I sat in a small, wooden chair by the piano, Hortense said that Jesus loved me, for the Bible told me so.

But at age twenty-eight, that all felt so . . . abstract. If indeed people communicate in love languages, I couldn't sense that God was speaking mine at all. How does an unseen God communicate with a mortal? I would, of course, first need to be convinced that He actually existed.

I preferred validation that I could hold in my hands— the steering wheel of a new car, a front-page news story, a brand-name purse, gilded writing awards to hang on my wall.

Now, *that* was approval. That was my love language, and I had learned to speak it fluently in the newsroom.

About one year before I sat in that limo with Al Gore, my editor asked if I would consider replacing David Yepsen, our newspaper's illustrious and widely regarded chief political correspondent. Yepsen had been praised as "one of the premier political writers in the country."

The late Illinois senator Paul Simon had high praise for Yepsen and for the position he held. "Every four years the chief political reporter for the *Des Moines Register* becomes the most important reporter in the nation," Simon wrote.[2]

To be sure, this promotion would mean higher-profile stories. I secretly suspected it would give me more of that clout I desired. My peers and parents would approve. My college professors would be impressed.

I would matter.

Reflecting on it all these years later, I can practically feel the Love Idol breathing down my neck.

One of my colleagues warned me against taking the job. He pulled me aside in my cubicle. After we sat down, he leaned his elbows on his knees. "Don't do it," my colleague told me. He reminded me that Yepsen was staying on staff as an opinion columnist and would probably scoop me on my own stories. What source would give the story to the twentysomething reporter when the gray-at-the-temples veteran was sitting in the same newsroom?

I heard the words but had different ideas. I would make up for my lack of gravitas by working more hours, producing more stories, scooping Yepsen if I had to. I didn't want to displease the editor who had asked, and I didn't want to forgo the opportunity to get more of what I was hungry for: validation and visible proof that my life mattered in the world.

The day came when, over lunch, I needed to give the editor my answer.

"Yes, I am willing," I told him as we dined at an eatery near the shimmering dome of the Iowa State Capitol.

This was it. This right here. I got what I wanted. I had bragging rights. Someone pop the champagne cork. I had stepped into the American dream. This is what our culture said would bring happiness.

Why, then, didn't I feel more satisfied each evening when I drove along the long, asphalt strips under the purplish glow of streetlights leading me home, with the echo of praise fading in my ears? Why do we always feel empty so soon after reaching some new pinnacle on whatever ladder we're climbing in this life?

On the outside, it might appear that you are living a rewarding life. But inside? Maybe you've felt as miserable as I did, despite the outward indicators.

I had no idea how to stop feeding this monster, which demanded more from me in order to be satisfied. I needed more page-one stories, more of the best assignments, more of the framed awards. My invisible standards were always elusive like that. Just when I thought I'd reached the top, I looked up and found that someone had, indeed, moved my cheese.

I didn't yet realize that this was a spiritual problem with a biblical answer.

In the limo, elbow-to-elbow with real clout, my practiced poise shrouded all of my quivering nervousness. I quizzed Al Gore on recent polls, an upcoming debate with George W. Bush, his immigration policy ideas, and his choice for a running mate.

Just as we pulled onto the tarmac, where Air Force Two waited, I asked the one question that wasn't on my prepared list. Out of nowhere came this: "What's your favorite Bible verse?"

I had read about immigration policy and scrutinized the latest polls, but it had been—what?—months since I last cracked open the Scriptures. And now I had the nerve to ask the vice president what his favorite verse was, hoping to catch him with his tongue tied?

Mr. Gore mentioned something about the Beatitudes. And I only nodded and scribbled down a few more notes. I sat there blinking, stunned—I, the fool. Because I was unable to remember even one of the Beatitudes.

That night, I went home and found my Bible where it lay as a dusty decoration on my nightstand. I flipped to the Beatitudes in Matthew 5. And I couldn't stop staring at those words about humility. I couldn't stop thinking about what those words might mean, and how they made no sense at all in my life, and how they represented nothing that I'd come to believe about a woman's significance in this world:

God blesses those who are humble,
     for they will inherit the whole earth. (Matthew 5:5)

What in the world could that ever mean?

.... ⌒⌒ ....

What demands does your Love Idol make of you?

CHAPTER 3

CONVICTION

No one in history had more titles than Jesus, or cared less.

BOB GOFF

I STOOD BAREFOOT in my kitchen, drumming fingers on the counter while waiting for two slices of whole wheat bread to spring from the toaster.

I was ready for this. At least that's what I told myself in grim situations like these, where the specter of death hooked one long, bony finger under my chin and forced me to look him in the eye. I set my jaw, clenched my teeth, and tried not to blink during stare-downs with the grave.

My black briefcase sat on the braided rug by the back door, next to my polished heels. The briefcase held four Steno pads, a handful of ballpoint pens, directions to the Indiana federal prison, and a thick stack of papers that included an "execution protocol fact card." Stapled documents fattened one manila folder. I had dashed a single inked word across the folder's tab: McVeigh.

A man by that name would die the next morning, before breakfast, under orders of the court.

Two pieces of bread popped out of the thin slots of my toaster. I buttered my toast, then left home for a deathwatch.

Death is daily business for a news reporter, the kind of spookish thing you try to swallow down calmly with your coffee every morning. Reporters follow that ghastly specter's footprints through tornado-strewn towns, war-torn villages, and bullet-riddled neighborhoods. In our newspaper, all deceased persons earned newsprint, not just the unfortunate ones whose bodies were outlined with crime-scene chalk. Every single mortal in our readership got a few short paragraphs on the obituary page, in the end, to mark a life.

And this was my life, consumed with death. And death, and death, and more of it . . . stacking up around me like all kinds of ghastly dry bones and overstuffed manila folders.

I wanted to find meaning in this life, but I couldn't find it among the big news stories, the accolades, and the trappings of success. Weeks earlier, I had been named "Young Iowa Journalist of the Year" and had received the "Outstanding Achievement Award" for writing from the media company Gannett. But the praise of man would not fill me.

I suppose I had read the words a few times in one of our church's pew Bibles as a teenager, how everything is a loss compared to knowing Christ.[1] Paul wrote that, though I'm not entirely sure I could have told you that at the time. Besides, you can read something—maybe even memorize it—but not really know it in your marrow. There's a difference. I was only beginning to learn it.

I did know some things. Like how lethal injection worked:

Sodium Pentothal, to render McVeigh unconscious.

Pancuronium bromide, to collapse his lungs.

Potassium chloride, to stop his heart.[2]

It would take less than ten minutes.

In twenty-four hours, Timothy McVeigh would be a dead man, at age thirty-three. This was court-ordered punishment for bombing the Oklahoma City federal building six years earlier. The blast killed 168 people. McVeigh held the distinction of being the nation's most notorious terrorist. (The September 11 attacks, which would forever change the nation's experience of terrorism on our own soil, were still three months and one day away.)

And I was the Iowa reporter assigned the task of driving to the federal penitentiary in Terre Haute, Indiana, to cover the event. The *Des Moines Register* didn't send reporters to every execution, but this national story had a connection to our city.

Jim McCarthy, the brother of Des Moines Assistant Police Chief Bill McCarthy, was killed in the bombing. And now, Bill would witness the lethal injection. Bill McCarthy was one of ten relatives and victims selected by lottery to watch McVeigh take his final breath. The McCarthys were our "local angle."

According to the federal prison's press kit, ten news reporters would also "have the opportunity" to witness the execution, sitting in a separate viewing room near McCarthy and the others.

Opportunity.

That was the single word that leaped at me in Times New Roman font, typed by some federal public-affairs agent in an Indiana cubicle. I wondered if he understood what he was typing when he chose that one word for the press release. Days before I left for Indiana, my editor dropped the press kit on my desk. It wasn't my editor's mandate that I sign up to be selected as one of the press-pool witnesses. And it wouldn't have been cause for termination if I had declined. But certainly everyone assumed that I would jump at the opportunity.

What journalist wouldn't want to see history made? Another notch in the reporter's belt. Another bit of glory. A glittery line on the résumé. Another great story to tell friends at the fifteen-year class reunion. "Hey, let me tell you about the time I watched a man die in federal prison." Sure, I would couch it in nicer terms, reminding others and myself that it was my honor-bound duty as a reporter to take the tough assignments. I could have made it sound like a sacrifice even. An earlier version of myself would have rehearsed the lines and everything.

But things were changing inside of me, a palpable turning. It was a slow spiritual revolution; I knew that. It had been happening for months now. Some people talk about "finding God," but that seemed like a severely inaccurate description of what I was experiencing. It felt more like God was finding me. He wasn't the lost one—I was.

I left the house for Indiana before dawn, driving into the eastern horizon. I watched the sunlight slide upward over a silo, a soybean field, and the silhouette of a barn. The sun shone like a promise, spilling gold rays over all that it touched. I flipped the visor down, shielding my eyes.

I swallowed hard, trying to keep emotion from rising up in my burning throat. I put my hand on my belly, which had begun to swell with new life. This would be her mother's legacy? To witness a terrorist's death? This would be what I was known for, a byline at a deathwatch? Would I really take my unborn child into an execution chamber for a front-row seat to death?

I swallowed again, trying to push back tears. Something was getting in the way of the only me I had known.

I kept one hand on my expanding midsection, longing to feel life moving on a day piled in death. My favorite handbook on all-things-pregnancy, *What to Expect When You're Expecting*, said that a first-time mother should be able to feel light movements around this time, or at least within a few weeks. My sisters had told me those first little twinges would feel like butterflies doing ballet in my belly.

Today, I wanted to think about butterflies in ballet slippers. I wanted to feel something metabolic.

I steered onto the interstate exit ramp as the Dixie Chicks sang through the speakers of my Camry. I pushed a button on the stereo to flip over to the AM dial and find my new favorite companion on long road trips: Christian talk radio.

Long-distance news assignments had lately afforded me uninterrupted stretches of idle time. I wanted to escape my own thoughts, even my own music. I was drawn to the intriguing messages coming from the voices on Christian talk radio. I don't remember the names that belonged to those voices now, but I do remember the beginnings of an inner turning. I was starting to believe. It was one of those mustard-seed-size faiths that I'd read about. Small, yes. But still, an inner light had begun to illumine my life, like that golden orb gliding up the eastern sky.

For years, I had secretly harbored doubts about the faith of my childhood. Those doubts were a long time festering, first emerging in my teenage years, even as I wrote the words "God is love" into my yellow notebook at age sixteen. I was afraid of dying, because deep down I worried that all life ended at the grave. I would later learn that doubt often tortured people of great faith—even Mother Teresa.[3] But at the time, I felt only shame over my doubt, a troubling sense that God might not exist at all. I also felt confusion, because my private pleas for God to reveal Himself were met only with a bitter silence.

Over the course of history, these have been the moments

when people whip up their own little idols. In our small minds, God seems distant or disinterested. We lose patience, and we begin to seek love and approval from more tangible gods. When God's presence isn't obvious to us, we are tempted to fashion idols out of what's right in front of us— what we can see and touch.

Take Aaron, for instance. The Israelites got antsy when Moses took so long to come down from the mountain, so they stomped their feet, demanding that Aaron give them some gods shaped to their liking. Aaron relented. He asked for every gold earring dangling from every single earlobe in the shadow of that mountain. Aaron "took what they handed him,"[4] melted it down, and molded it into an idol shaped like a calf.

These days, idols aren't usually shaped like farm animals. But, like Aaron, we make idols out of what we hold in our hands.

My doubts about God triggered the molding of my very own Love Idol. And as the idol grew bigger, it increasingly blocked God's love from my field of vision.

My doubts intensified during my years as a student at Iowa State University. And they were fully raging by the time I married Scott, my college sweetheart, in 1996 under a small-town steeple.

I wanted to believe the faith of my childhood. I really did. But I couldn't. God felt like a fairy tale, and it was foolish to believe in fairy tales. Yet I didn't want to admit my doubts publicly, to my family or close friends, who seemed to hold fast to the faith.

My husband was the only human who had any idea of my doubts, and I suppose it's because I no longer felt the need to seek his approval or impress him by pretending otherwise. I knew that he loved me because he loved me. I didn't realize it yet, but that kind of acceptance foreshadowed the love I'd find in a Savior—an unrelenting love that doesn't depend one iota on my gold-star performance.

One night early in our marriage, angled knee-to-knee under the covers, I leaked out my doubt, whispering into the inky darkness: "Scott, do you ever have trouble believing?"

My husband only said, "No, I don't." Then he rolled over to fall asleep. Years later, I would ask him why his answer was so clipped. He told me he believed in God but wasn't interested in a surrendered life, because he wasn't sure what that would mean for his own performance-based, approval-soaked lifestyle as a law-school graduate and hard-charging businessman.

So my question hung in the air for years, as we both internally pondered what it meant.

I stuffed my doubts out of sight—like they were some kind of failure—not wanting to admit them to my parents, my Sunday school teachers, my Christian friends. I certainly wouldn't want to confess doubt to a pastor. I was a great pretender, occasionally even attending religious services for appearances' sake. My husband attended too. But one thing we didn't know yet about God's Word was this: When the Word goes out from God's mouth, "it always produces fruit" (Isaiah 55:11).

Fruit grew, not so much like a plump, juicy watermelon, but like a few small blueberries here and there. We had a hunch that this was what we'd been missing. We began to sense that this was why we had felt so empty, even though outside indicators would suggest we were getting along swimmingly in this approval-saturated culture. We wouldn't fully learn until later that our hunger after the American dream could be one way to actually *starve*. People can be fooled into thinking they can live on their own good performances and approval ratings. But they need real Bread.

I was beginning to get a taste of this new kind of nourishment on talk radio and in Sunday morning worship services, which we began to attend with more regularity. I had never heard of the sinner's prayer until I started listening to Christian talk radio. After hearing about it, I prayed the prayer numerous times over a series of months, thinking that if saying it once was good, saying it fifty times was even better. This may seem like a fumbling, stumbling, bad-theology movement toward God, but there you have it. This was the messy way that I got acquainted with my Savior.

I began to memorize verses. Bible stories took on new meaning for my own life.

But it was far more than what *I* did. The Holy Spirit was actively doing a real, transforming work inside of me. There was no other explanation. I was drawn to Christian

talk radio by an inexplicable hunger. I did not listen out of
a sense of obligation. It felt like life pooling up between all
these dry bones.

It began to occur to me on those long drives toward
anywhere that maybe I had actually tuned out whole sec-
tions of Sunday school. A soul can instinctively know what
Blaise Pascal pointed out: "There is a God-shaped vacuum
in the heart of every man which cannot be filled by any
created thing, but only by God, the Creator, made known
through Jesus."[5]

I also began to learn quickly that my mind was inca-
pable of multitasking thoughts. Whenever I thought about
Jesus Christ as Savior, as He was being described through
my car's speakers, I couldn't think about myself so much.
When I looked upward, I couldn't look inward at the same
time. Both eyes had to look in the same direction. I liked
that. I didn't have to concern myself with my performance
but could focus on the performance of a Savior, who
Christian talk-show hosts said had died for me while I
was yet a sinner.[6]

All of that felt holy and right and true. And I would
need to remember how it felt. I'd need to remember it
those times when the bony fingers of the world curled
under my chin, begging me to look.

McVeigh was to die at 7 a.m. by lethal injection in the execution chamber of the US Penitentiary in Terre Haute,

Indiana. I arrived the afternoon before, so I could cover the events leading up to the execution.

As I drove down the road toward the prison, I felt like I was on the midway at the state fair. People were outside the prison grounds selling twenty-five-cent lemonades and shish kebabs. Others hawked T-shirts. Protesters were picnicking at the roadside. News reporters were "carrying it live," sharing death with a worldwide audience. They were all there: ABC, CBS, FOX, NBC, CNN, Reuters.[7]

This was how America participated in the dizzying deathwatch of a terrorist. And I had just become a part of this macabre spectacle—me, this mama-to-be with spiral-bound notebooks in a black briefcase.

I pulled my Camry into a yard about a quarter mile from the prison, where a guy named Tedd was selling $25 parking spaces on his sister's lawn. I grabbed my notebook and my press credentials, along with my parking fee for Tedd.

"It's the American way," Tedd said with a shrug. He was holding a clipboard and carrying a wad of cash in his pocket. I pressed my payment into his hand, then asked if I could interview him. I took notes, furiously writing down every word. "We're reaping the profits. This is everybody's fifteen minutes of fame, you know what I mean?"[8]

Yeah, I knew what he meant. I bought a cup of lemonade from his eleven-year-old niece. I smiled at her, a smile that I didn't feel on the inside. I tried to keep the lemonade down.

The spin of fame made me queasy.

What was my fifteen minutes of fame worth, anyway? What would this cost me? How would I record this one in the baby book?

I walked in the general direction of the press-briefing area, a slow walk with one hand holding my notepad and another on my belly, like a shield. I interviewed people along the way, protestors and pastors and entrepreneurs raking in the dough with their food stands and T-shirt sales.

And then it was time to sign up, with my press credentials, for that once-in-a-lifetime chance to see the killing of a killer. Ten seats were available for news media. None of us were guaranteed a seat; each would be selected by lottery.

I don't know how close I was to finding the sign-up sheet when it happened. It felt like the whole planet suddenly shifted, like I might lose my balance on a federal-prison sidewalk. I wanted to muffle my ears from all the protesting and chanting. I couldn't stand to look at another Sharpie'd poster board on a stick, another microphoned reporter sending the story back home.

My feet stopped moving. I stood under the late-afternoon sun, near the prison, feeling like another kind of prisoner. Then I made my move. I turned around and headed back to the yard where my car was parked. I drove to my hotel room a few miles away. I needed to be small, quiet. I checked into my hotel room to file the story of McVeigh's last day alive, as I'd been instructed to do. Then I went to bed and did something that I'd only really begun to do. I prayed. It was a feeble prayer, but I prayed it anyway: "Lord. Just. I don't know. Just help me."

I couldn't do it. I couldn't watch that man die. I did not sign up for the "opportunity" of a lifetime. Other reporters could and would do it. And I didn't fault them. I still don't. The press's watchdog role over government functions—even the most grisly ones—is an important duty in a democracy. But I knew that, this time, I couldn't stomach the task.

I drew the heavy drapes, curled under the bedsheet in a darkened room, and slept better than I had in weeks, lulled to sleep by the drone of a hotel-room air conditioner.

The next morning, I arrived at the prison grounds just before McVeigh was escorted into the execution chamber. I stood outside, looking up at the coiled razor wire, wondering briefly if I should lie to my editor when I returned to the newsroom. I could tell him that I had signed up as a witness but that my name hadn't been drawn, or that I didn't get there in time to submit my credentials. But I decided I would tell him the truth. I was tired of lies, including the ones I told myself.

While the execution witnesses gathered inside the prison, I waited outside for an hour or more under that blue sky on press row, lined with TV trucks. I stood on the free side, knowing this: Too often in my life, I'd said yes to things I didn't really want to do—for fear of disappointing someone, for fear of looking like a failure.

But sometimes, a woman has to risk her approval rating by saying no.

Inside the prison, a death was about to happen. I would gather all the facts for my story after the witnesses came out and spoke into the microphone, standing on a stage set up on the prison's front lawn.

Before the execution, the warden asked McVeigh if he had any final words, but he remained silent. Rather than make his remarks aloud, McVeigh had given the warden a handwritten statement in which he quoted from a nineteenth-century poem: "I am the master of my fate: I am the captain of my soul."[9]

Then the injection snaked through his body.

At 7:14 a.m. on a Monday morning, Timothy McVeigh was pronounced dead.

I met with the McCarthys at a park a short while later. "This is the end of a chapter," McCarthy said.

And I felt it too—my own kind of death, a closing of a chapter. On the drive home, someone on Christian radio used the phrase "dying to self." I wondered if that's what was happening inside of me. I was not, after all, the captain of my soul.

I steered my way home, unashamed, like I was driving to an altar, a place to lay down my own will and the American dream and that ridiculous chase for some shred of personal glory. I would face criticism at home, not praise. Friends who worked at a competing paper would mock me. There would be no gilded, framed award for this lackluster act of reportage. In the newsroom, it would reek of cowardice.

So be it. I had decided.

.... ᗉᗆ ....

In what ways does your Love Idol fail to satisfy you?

CHAPTER 4

MUD PIES

Whatever your heart clings to and confides in,
that is really your God, your functional savior.

MARTIN LUTHER

A HOSPITAL MONITOR BEEPED. The blood-pressure cuff
tightened around my arm. And a five-pound girl with a
striped beanie on her head exhaled in short, warm breaths
against my neck. My husband dozed while curled on the
two-cushion couch pushed up against the opposite wall.

This tiny miracle skidded into the world three weeks
early, but right on time. God had sent two babies to shake
up my life—one in a Bethlehem manger and another in a
hospital maternity ward. And I had only begun to get
acquainted with both of them.

Which, of course, meant that I was slowly getting to
know myself.

The CNN news ticker on the TV in the corner of my hospital room told me that a device called the Xbox had been unveiled that day. Analysts talked about the economic ripple effects of the World Trade Center attacks, which had occurred two months earlier. And my college friend and former news colleague Christine Romans appeared on the screen, giving viewers a rundown of the day's financial news.

There would be no Jennifer Dukes Lee bylines today.

As a journalist, I had chased news stories for years, while keeping the Good News—the very best news story—sealed between the dust-caked covers of my Bible. But I had begun to feel a new pull toward Scripture. I read the book with wonder. God reintroduced me to actual *people* in the Bible. I had first met them when I was a kid. Back then, they were outlined figures, reduced to Sunday school coloring pages: Paul, John, Matthew, Mary, Martha. And a woman named Lydia, a seller of purple cloth.

In the hospital bed, I brushed my lips back and forth across my firstborn's soft cheek, whispering in her ear, "I love you, Little Miss Lydia."

Luke wrote of the biblical Lydia, "The Lord opened her heart" (Acts 16:14).

God had been opening my heart too. It felt more like a sacred swelling, like the good Lord was occupying that hollow ache of space under my ribs. I cradled my baby against my skin, praying for her as I memorized each tiny crease, eyelash, and sigh. Every square inch of her declared that God cared enough about people to keep sending more of us here.

The blanket-cocooned newborn in my arms wriggled. As I held her close, I remembered how we all come into this world wanting to be loved. Back on Groundhog Day in 1972, a nurse pulled a striped beanie over my pointy little head. I cried for someone to hold me, someone to love and care for me. People never outgrow that God-designed craving for love.

But where would my child seek love? Would she think love might be found in her own good performances, the applause, her social status, the American dream, a perfect report card, a pair of designer shoes, the right car, a manipulative boyfriend, or her parents' pats on the back? How might history fold over on itself?

I closed my eyes, wishing that Lydia might know that she was God's good idea all along, loved immeasurably more than any of the sorry substitutes the world would eventually hold out to her.

My wishes felt like prayers. And the baby whimpered, wanting to be fed.

While on maternity leave, I submitted my resignation to the newspaper's editor.

There would be no more press releases. No more limo rides or front-page scoops. I didn't know if I'd ever write again.

I didn't need another byline; I needed a lifeline.

This was the year we decided to move back to the family

farm—the farm where my husband, Scott, grew up in the far northwest corner of Iowa. This new life was not the one I had envisioned for myself. In fact, I once vowed in an essay I'd written for the *Des Moines Register*'s opinion page that I would "never again live in my rural hometown."

True enough, I didn't move back to *my* hometown. But we were moving back to Scott's. It was a small town with no stoplights, eight hundred residents, one hardware store, and five churches. There were no billboards or marquees. If local folks wanted to announce a church soup supper or Kiwanis pancake breakfast, they tacked a handmade poster to a barrel and then rolled it right into the middle of Main Street.

We packed up all our furniture, my yellowing newspaper clippings, the framed awards, and my husband's law-school books. We duct-taped our lives in cardboard and moved north for a quieter existence among the tall corn and church spires.

Standing at the back end of our packed U-Haul, ready to head for a simple life on the farm, I thought, *Surely this is how a Christian woman might find peace and real fulfillment. She would move five hours away from the source of her approval, from her editors and readers and newsroom peers.* I would no longer be manhandled by my inner critic. I would not be swayed by the opinions of others. I would lick this propensity for approval-seeking all by my brave little self. Yes, this move would change everything.

I'm guessing you know how that worked: Yeah . . . *No.* It didn't work. Not even a little.

I would learn that personal hang-ups are like parasites;

they are stubborn pests, continuing to feed on their hosts if left untreated. If the host moves to a new home, so does the parasite. I brought my parasitic baggage straight up that long country lane, right behind the U-Haul.

Before I'd unpacked the last box, I wondered how the local community would react to the city girl who had come home to her husband's family farm. I assumed I would be the outsider in a community full of lifelong insiders, where everyone knew everyone else by name—and by their pickup trucks. I believed that I would be only "Scott's wife" to the locals.

I had noble roles as a mother and a wife. But I felt fully unqualified to be a *farm*wife. With our move, Scott had become the fourth-generation Lee farmer to glean these fields. And thus, I became the fourth-generation Lee farm-wife. The women who came before me were Emma, Eunice, and Joyce, my mother-in-law. But one of these Lee wives was not like the others. (That one would be me.) The other Lee women knew how to bake and can vegetables. They could sew and garden. I made brick-hard brownies and the world's flattest angel food cake. I knew nothing about bobbins or blanket stitches. I generally avoided such activities, knowing they held inherent risks for a woman like me. (I might get my own shirt mixed in with the project and end up sewing myself to the machine.)

After we moved home, my husband and father-in-law would talk about farming at the dinner table. They would go on about grain markets or the price of a combine. I'd quietly chew my roast beef and spoon pureed peas into Lydia's tiny bird-mouth. I nodded my head as if I understood the adult discussion, but I contributed nothing. Once upon a time, I had asked good questions and made intelligent contributions to conversations. People had returned my calls. Where was my Rolodex now anyway?

I wanted to know that I mattered. I had not yet come to terms with the spiritual reality that, in Christ, I did matter. I still liked people more than God. I still wanted people's approval more than His. The editors and professors and colleagues in my life were replaced with another set of people whose approval I sought: my new neighbors and a whole group of local women who—I assumed— actually *knew* how to be farmwives. I was, as one farmer told me at the county fair, "a real fish out of water."

I wanted to fit in. I missed the respect I'd once had. I was no better off here than I'd been in the city. I might have been worse. I would have been in the target audience for John 12:43: "They loved human praise more than the praise of God."

Lydia celebrated her first birthday in our brand-new home with its faux-stone facade. After the cake was eaten and the house was emptied of guests, I sat with Lydia on the floor of her nursery. That big, new house held too much quiet, and the clock ticked much too loudly in the next room. Lydia's pudgy little hands gripped her *Goodnight Moon* board book. She turned the book's cardboard pages, softened at the corners from all her gumming. Lydia had made a game of looking for the white mouse hidden on each page. Her eyes swept across the open book, and at last she spotted the white mouse, frozen forever on the book's red carpet by the fireplace logs. She plopped her forefinger on top of it, then turned her face to grin at me. My chin quivered.

And who doesn't weep for the fullest life? Who, among us all, doesn't ache for more? What would it take for me to finally understand that the fullest life isn't tied to the temporal?

I don't think I could have put a finger on it yet. I couldn't quite find the hidden, white mouse on the carpet of my life. But I see it now, looking back: I still craved fulfillment from people. I craved it more than I craved God. I longed for fulfillment, but where would I go hunting for it? If I'm honest, I still figured that the hollow ache in my center would be assuaged the way it always had been: by someone giving me an "attagirl."

True, I'd had one conversion, from unbelief to Christ belief. But I needed a second conversion, from bondage to freedom. I had yet to lay hold of the fullness of my salvation. And I didn't yet know how to fight those inner wars.

It would take years before I would learn that a simple change of address from city to farm was not the path toward freedom. The problem wasn't the newsroom. The problem was the news*woman*. This is the bold truth: You can't run away from your problems in some maddening search for peace. Peace has never been about a place. It has always been about a Person.

But I had not yet come to the end of myself, where Christ Jesus was waiting all along.

Until you are convinced of God's incredible love for you, you will continue looking for replacement love everywhere but in the heart of Christ.

No matter where you live or work, temptation confronts you. The enemy prowls around like a lion, stalking people on Wall Street, fashion runways, suburban cul-de-sacs, Facebook walls, and even gravel roads in rural Iowa. You and I are in a showdown with Satan, who will use every opportunity he can to whisper in our ears, "What are people thinking of you?"[1]

The enemy will tell you that you're too fat, too frumpy, too stupid, too poor. He will do whatever he can to set your affections on the things of this world, instead of on Christ. And he'll wrap those accusations in glossy magazine covers if he has to.

Our culture is hawking approval, and it's a multibillion-dollar business. The search for approval might lead some women to crash dieting, hoping that if only they looked better, someone they love might finally notice them. It might lead others to chase after more friends, followers, and fans to feed a growing appetite to be known among people. Some might clamor for the respect and admiration of people in the inner circle. Others might abandon personal convictions in favor of popularity. We gain the world, but at what cost?

We get our fill, and then—*poof*—it is gone. For what end? Love idols rust. In a blink, this life will be over. And our popularity ratings will mean nothing on the other side of eternity. We have to ask ourselves now, starting today and every day, *Whose "attagirl" am I after? Whom do I really want to say, "Well done"?*

The implications are not only personal but global. If your need for more and more approval apart from God builds, it might distract you from your earthly calling entirely. You might miss what God has for you. Here's why: The Holy Spirit might nudge you to take a new job, adopt a child, move to the mission field, become a Sunday school teacher, start a Bible study, or write a book. But if you're looking over your shoulder, wondering what people think of you, you might be inclined to ignore that nudge. You might walk away from your call, your God-designed purpose for living, because you are afraid. You fear dis-approval and rejection, so you turn your back on the very mission God has called you to.

I have been guilty of ignoring nudges. I have been a modern-day Much-Afraid.[2]

But I have also been loved and gently guided. Even as I struggled to find my truest identity in Christ, the Holy Spirit, like a consummate gentleman, escorted me straight into the Word of God.

During those lonely first years on the farm, I began asking some questions: *What does the Bible say about this? What does it really mean to be approved?*

I found one powerful answer in 2 Timothy 2:15: "Work hard so you can present yourself to God and receive his approval."

Not so I could present myself to newspaper readers. Or peers. Or parents. Or neighbors. Or even Bible study partners and pastors.

"Work hard so you can present yourself *to God* and receive *his* approval."

But retraining my eyes toward Christ would take years—and might, in fact, take a whole lifetime.

After moving to the farm, our family grew by one more baby. Anna's arrival upped the stakes again. My husband and I wanted both of our girls to know what love really meant.

Many years later, I flew to Haiti. During that trip, I made a startling discovery in a village. A local woman had mixed dirt with oil, then pressed the mixture into tiny discs that looked like cookies. She had lined hundreds of these mud-cookies on mats, where they were drying out in the sun. After the discs were thoroughly dried, these dirt cakes would be eaten. *By people.* This was not some bizarre Haitian delicacy. People in Haiti eat dirt because it gives their starving bodies a false sense of satisfaction.

But mud pies don't fill. They merely mask real hunger.

I snapped a photograph of those mud pies, and at first glance, I saw them as a depressing truth about world hunger and abject poverty. Later, I saw the mud pies as a metaphor for the life of any Christian who has ever looked to something or someone other than God for fulfillment.

We can go whole lifetimes eating mud pies. I ate a lot of dirt before even trying the Bread of Life.

Now I want more Bread, less dirt. I want more life, less mud. I want the love for which my hunger was created.

And if you've come this far with me, you do too.

At times, this fight can feel like an inner war. The Bible is our sword; the Prince of Peace, our captain. A whole cloud of witnesses is cheering us on, and the saints know how this one ends.

My husband, my daughters, and I are still on this farm. Our girls are now in grade school; both are tempted by all the mud pies of the world, in places like soccer fields, magazine covers, and spelling-bee stages. They have begun to experience the pressure to perform and perfect. But my husband and I want them to know how they are *already* loved by a Savior. We want to know it ourselves.

And we want you to know it too.

We are all worth fighting for. On Calvary, Jesus said as much. But because Christ has us for eternity, the enemy is doing all that he can to undermine us while we're on earth.

So comes this story. This fight for glory. This war.

Let's do this.

Has your Love Idol ever convinced you to move to a different address, take a different job, or hang out with a different crowd? What was the result?

CHAPTER 5

BEE STING

Fear camps out right next to whatever it is you're most called
to do. That means the closer you get to your calling,
the louder fear sounds. . . . Keep going—fear is
a Chihuahua that sounds like a Doberman.

HOLLEY GERTH

IT's 8 A.M. on a Monday. Mellow morning sunlight slants
through my kitchen window overlooking the Iowa farm
fields. My daughter Lydia presses open a brochure on the
breakfast table, and she taps a determined finger on the
printed words—Lyon County Fair Spelling Bee—before
pushing the flyer toward me.

"I want to try this year, Mommy."

I add milk to her Cap'n Crunch, noticing that she's
already turned to read the nutrition panel on the cereal
box. She stirs and reads, stirs and reads. Her face tenses
with focus, like some wizened old man hunched over the
morning paper. Her daddy's corn crop has stretched past

the telltale marker: knee-high-by-the-Fourth-of-July. For most children, this is the season of Popsicles, pink shoulders, and kites set adrift on summer skies. But this child? She studies.

I wonder if she might be memorizing words like *polyunsaturated* and *riboflavin* while churning her Cap'n Crunch in a soggy circle.

I rest my chin on my hand and study her. I know her look. I've perfected it over these thirty-some years. The similarities between mother and daughter are uncanny.

Her hair appears to have been parted with an X-Acto knife. This girl reads the cereal box the same way I used to, devouring syllables because you never know when memorized words might need to be pressed into service.

I flip open the county fair's brochure and review the lists of contests and competitions. They look so harmless. Yet such things carry inherent risks for girls like her, for grown-ups like me.

If my daughter loses, she might never try again. But if she wins, she'll be fed more praise for her performance. She'll climb one rung higher on the glory ladder, making her eventual fall that much more painful.

What a dangerous thing, a spelling bee.

Then again, maybe I'm overthinking things. I do wonder. I brush crumbs from the polished pine table. She has waited a year for this.

Last year, on a whim, it was I who suggested Lydia sign up for the county fair spelling bee. She is a terrific speller, having mastered words like *encyclopedia* and *premature* back in the first grade. But when we arrived at the registration table, a woman with her hair pulled into a tight, gray knot sized my daughter up quickly.

"How old?" she asked.

"She'll be a third grader this fall."

The woman shook her head. "Sorry, but she'll have to wait until she's a fourth grader."

Lydia vowed to return one year later, one year smarter, with more memorized words in her noggin.

I had forgotten about that moment until now. Lydia, apparently, had not.

And so, on a July afternoon, we drive the twenty-five miles to the fair, past cornfields waving their happy, green greeting. I hear my daughter spelling out our route.

"Tractor. T-R-A-C-T-O-R. Tractor."

"H-I-G-H-W-A-Y."

"C-A-T-T-L-E."

As she spells, my mind wanders, and I remember a spot-lighted stage where I once stood among one hundred of our region's finest young spellers. I was a fifth grader, as I remember it. It's grainy on the playback, so I don't remember the word, but I do remember this: It was a three-letter word, and I'd never heard it before. I was eliminated from the district spelling bee in the first round of competition.

Never mind that earlier I'd earned rights to that stage by winning two other competitions. Nothing mattered but this: I was knocked from the spotlight by two consonants and a vowel. Humiliated, I cried for the next hour in one of those padded, fold-down auditorium chairs. I had weighed the costs well before taking the stage. Even at age ten, I built up big events in my mind and then panicked over my potential failure. When we bomb in our performances, girls like me vow never to try again.

I steer the car into the fairgrounds' parking lot and find a space near a barn full of sheep, all bleating staccato. My girl and I walk through the barns, trimmed with blue and red ribbons from the 4-H livestock shows held earlier that day.

We hold hands as we walk. I choose our steps carefully—you never know what you might step on, here in a cattle barn. I choose my words with the same prudence: "Lydia? Have you thought that you might not win? Are you okay with that?"

The Holsteins, Herefords, and Simmentals are bellowing, a lively chorus of bassists.

She rolls her eyes. "I know, Mom."

I begin to wonder if I'm offering cautionary advice for her benefit or for my own. Do I secretly want her to win? As a mom, I am never altogether sure of my motives.

I know, I know. We're heading to a county spelling bee, not a medical board exam. But I also recognize the ugliest parts of me, the parts that I try to hide behind my good

performance. I want to *do* well because I want someone
to *say* I've done well. That feels like love to me.

A few weeks earlier, I needed some clarification on the
roots of my struggle. Sherri, a psychology professor at the
Christian college where I teach journalism, said we could
meet off campus at Butler's coffee shop for lunch. We
huddled over steaming soup bowls at a table near the back.
I dropped my forehead onto one hand. How, I asked, can a
believer struggle with something she so clearly knows is sin?

"Look, it's just misdirected love," Sherri said, stirring her
bowl of vegetable soup. "Your desire to be loved comes from
a good place, from a God place even." She lifted her spoon
to her mouth.

"All right then," I said. "But why do believers sometimes
care more about what humans think than what God
thinks? Why do I live like that at times? It's not my inten-
tion, but . . ."

She set down her spoon and folded her arms on the table.
"Sin has distorted our deepest needs. It's not just you."

I know Sherri's right. I've counseled students who've
struggled with perfectionism, negative body image, and
a sense that they aren't fitting in—all of which affect their
ability to recognize their true identity in Christ. They
know the scriptural answers about their worth, but they
still crave accolades from their peers and professors.

That craving follows so many of us straight into
middle age.

Sherri said that, in essence, it's part of our human

condition. She reminded me how God paired Adam and Eve together in the Garden. God walked those curving paths with them by the river. And it was good. Then, when they thought their Maker wasn't paying attention, Adam and Eve sank their teeth into an apple—all for a chance to be like God. They figured their Creator was holding out; they didn't trust His love. The snake went hissing away, carrying our stolen innocence on his scale-covered back. With a single bite, our desire for love was twisted. And as the thief slithered into the grass, Adam and Eve went running for cover. They hid from God, and ever since then, people have been looking outside of Eden for something to fulfill that inner craving.

We are like Eve. We've distrusted God. We've been lured by an out-of-Eden placebo: human validation. We thought it would cure our ache for love. It never has.

Our lives bear the evidence: We are grown women, some of whom thrash in our bedsheets at 2 a.m., burdened with worry. Some of us have nursed ulcers. We've spent countless angst-filled hours replaying conversations at dinner parties, phone calls with friends, even passing remarks to our mothers-in-law. We second-guess. We fret, pointlessly really. We save too-small jeans, hoping that someday . . .

A.W. Tozer wrote of the "self-sins." His words hound me, all these decades later. At times I suffer from self-pity, self-doubt, self-condemnation, selfishness. And let me just call this need for approval what it is: another sin of the self.[1]

It makes me sad to admit it, but I have desired self-esteem over Christ-esteem.

Walking through the cattle barn, I glance down at my daughter, tiny heiress to my DNA. I worry that she suffers from the same affliction. She's only nine, but I see it in the way she cracks jokes for her friends. (She wants to be the funniest one.) I know how she frets over the possibility of an A-minus. (She wants to be the smartest one.) And I've counseled her when she tearfully recounts the game where she wore the goalie shirt and two balls slipped past her. (She wants to be the athletic one.)

Last semester, when she agonized over a social studies test, I did what I would have liked to have done for myself long ago: I dared her to get a B.

I don't always practice what I preach. I have begun to realize that even when I know the right answers, it's hard to live them. And until I'm ready to live them, they are only theoretical notions, good philosophy, words that would be *nice* to put into practice.

I worry, too, if I unwittingly project my expectations onto this little soul.

I know how we parents can act in competitive situations. I see it many Saturday mornings while sitting in a canvas lawn chair at the edge of a soccer field. There's usually a parent barking orders at little girls in shin guards. I sit in quiet indignation, thrusting my tongue in my cheek and finding some smug satisfaction in having my "priorities straight."

At halftime, I murmur reminders to my daughters that "having fun" is the priority. They're playing for sport, not for a trophy.

But when we trade soccer fields for spelling-bee stages, I elevate my expectations. Now, mind you, I wouldn't dream of growling at a child for misspelling a word. But if she messes up, will I secretly wish she had gotten it right? Is a spelling bee really "just for fun"?

Lydia and I walk out the south end of the cattle barn with our fingers laced. I notice a young boy about Lydia's age thumbtacking a purple ribbon to the wooden pen that fences in his prized cow. The words on the ribbon are imprinted in gold: Grand Champion.

All the world's a competition, it seems.

Lydia and I show up at the registration table, where the same gray-haired woman is signing in spellers. A long line of children has already formed.

When we reach the table, the woman sizes up my daughter, like she did a year earlier. "How old is she?"

I tell her she'll be a fourth grader. Lydia pushes her purple-rimmed glasses up the bridge of her nose with a single finger.

The woman says the spelling bee is for children who have *completed* the fourth grade. Lydia's shoulders droop. But— the woman pauses—perhaps she can participate, so long as she realizes she will be competing against children who are all one grade above her.

Done.

Lydia inks her name in cursive on the line, under fourteen other names.

She sees it first: the piece of paper Scotch-taped down at the other end of the table. It's a sign-in sheet for adult spellers. Lydia tugs my arm and begs me to try. But I shake my head firmly. I force a smile—the kind where you could grind the enamel off your back teeth. I tell my daughter that we've come here for *her*, and there's no sense waiting around all afternoon until the adults are called onto the stage. Besides, wouldn't she rather get home to jump on the trampoline? And this: We could get cotton candy on the way out.

I have her at cotton candy. We walk away from the table, and I am secretly relieved that I, a former news reporter, have escaped the potential embarrassment of screwing up in front of a live audience. I wince when I think of what might have happened if I'd been asked to spell one of those words that have always given me fits: "accommodate" or—believe it or not—"misspelled."

Lydia and I find a seat on a wooden bench toward the back. She asks me to review the spelling bee rules with her. I tell her that the pronouncer will say the word and use it in a sentence. I remind her that some words sound alike but are spelled differently: "Like flour that you use to make cookies and a flower that you pick from the garden."

I can see the color draining from her cheeks. I know this look: regret.

I put a hand on the small of her back. "You don't have to do this, honey."

"But I want to." Her eyes are rimmed pink and glistening. "I'm just scared, Mommy."

I recognize this as a teaching moment for daughter and mother.

I cup her hands in mine and ask her straight out: "What is the worst thing that could happen if you lose? If you don't even get second place? If . . . *you miss the first word?*"

A single tear falls down her cheek, and she brushes it away with her shoulder.

"Well," she says, "I guess we would just go home."

Precisely. The world would not end. We would just go home. I make a mental note of this. I will need to remember.

∼⎯⌖⎯∽

Another woman calls the children to the stage. Lydia stands up and lets out all her air in one long breath. Fourteen fourth graders—and one third grader—ascend the wooden stairs.

Lydia sits on her hands, at the far end of a bench onstage. She is staring straight at me, and I think she looks half-surprised that she has found herself up there. Just now, the woman hands her the microphone.

My daughter will be the first speller. She stands.

The word has four letters. But is it *heel* or *heal*? I watch Lydia as she listens to the definition. This is the moment where fear and hope collide. Win or lose, there's an audience. Either way, that's a dangerous thing.

This I know: These are the kind of teaching moments that frame a person's character, and I am the student most in need of learning.

I lean forward and whisper words. "It's okay. It's okay, honey."

It dawns on me: Part of me wants her to lose. I know this could serve as an important lesson—that a person actually does survive, even if she fails and the applause fades. She would find that her mother—and the Lord—approve of her simply because she exists, not because she performed flawlessly. So yes, a part of me hopes she'll lose. Another part of me feels like I'm betraying my own child with such a two-faced thought. I smile and give her a thumbs-up from across the room.

I remember what she said. I remember the only words that really matter anyway. She said the right words three minutes ago: "I guess we would just go home."

It stuns me, how I need to relearn simple lessons. *We go home when it's over.* Isn't this what we've preached? "Fix your eyes on Jesus," we tell our children. "Think on heaven, our forever home. Don't worry about who's watching. Do what you do for an Audience of One." Isn't this what matters most? Character over victory? God's praise over man's?

I want to live the right answers to my questions. I want to live what I believe, and in this moment, I'm painfully aware of the fact that I often don't.

I watch my daughter on the stage. She is the brave one. Who is teaching whom here? Mother or child? She is trying to swallow down fear, trying to push the letters past it.

And just like that—"Heel. H-E-E-L. Heel."—Lydia advances to round two.

She passes the microphone and, in a gesture of relief, gives me her own enthusiastic thumbs-up. A few in the crowd notice and politely laugh.

A boy misses his word. Then a girl. And two more boys. The pronouncer asks one child to spell *flour*—just like we'd practiced!—and an astonished grin stretches across Lydia's face. When she turns toward me, I see that the color has returned to her cheeks.

I mouth the single word: "Wow!"

Finally, after several rounds, only two girls are standing. One of them is Lydia.

The two girls advance through a series of words, again and again. The cheering crescendos signal the crowd's approval. (I am mildly annoyed with myself for noticing.)

At last, the other girl misses. She spells the place between mountains like this: "V-A-L-L-I-E-S."

Lydia takes the microphone, and the room falls quiet. "Valleys," she says. "V-A-L-L-E-Y-S. Valleys."

The audience swells with applause. Lydia has won. Someone hands her a prize in an envelope, and she smiles her thanks. She descends the steps and cuts through the crowd toward me. I see her beaming, waving a crisp ten-dollar bill that she has pulled from the envelope.

True enough, this child is the winner. But I wonder if the real victory came before the word *valleys* was spoken. Did I not witness true triumph, in that tearful valley thirty minutes ago, right here on a wooden bench?

It may seem like some small thing, a little spelling bee on a stage somewhere in Iowa, out where the corn tassels in mid-July and moms hang shirts on the line. But I know better. What this child did was no minor thing. In a fight-or-flight moment, she inked her name and climbed onto the stage. She risked failing, for the sheer joy of trying.

My own daughter makes me feel brave, makes me realize that I might be able to risk my own approval rating for the sake of fuller living. I'm feeling ready to dare myself to get a B, even—*gasp!*—a C. I want to live into the fullness of my salvation, not only for heaven but right here on Earth. Life trains our brains to resist anything that might make us look stupid. But I don't want fear to be the boss of me anymore.

The spelling-bee champion is running toward me now, clutching her reward. I stand up and spread my arms wide, leaning over to embrace my girl. And here, bending at the waist, I find myself in the posture of learning and relearning. Right here, hugging my child, I'm just beginning to see.

Perhaps it's not the annihilation of fear that is most important. It's ascending the steps in spite of it.

I draw her in close, knowing that it's time for both of us to start living what we believe. She seems to have gotten a head start. With my daughter in my arms, I remember a twenty-seven-year-old note, written on pink notebook paper.

In 1984, Mrs. Huseman pressed that note onto my desk.

"After all," the teacher wrote, "there always will be tomorrow."

Tomorrow has been a long time coming.

What might your Love Idol reveal about
your view of God and His ability or
willingness to provide for your needs?

CHAPTER 6

"GOD'S GOT IT"

There is only one love language. It's called "die to self."
CHRISTINE CAINE

HERE'S THE THING about the Love Idol: It thrusts its bossy self between you and God's call on your life.

And when that Love Idol gets up in your business, you can't quite hear what God is saying to you.

That Love Idol is downright stubborn. I want to be stubborn-er.

Because the moment we stop fussing over the opinions of others might be the moment we start actually living for God. Only then can we fearlessly love our neighbors, lead a Bible study, talk into a microphone, pray out loud, stand up for our beliefs, fight for the underdog, speak truth in love, write a book, or take audacious risks for the Kingdom.

I'm thinking about all that this morning as the sunlight begins to push back the dark blanket of the heavens. I sigh, burrowing deeper under the covers. In spite of my resolve to stand up to the Love Idol, doubts are already creeping in, making me question my ability to change lifelong patterns.

Maybe I am a coward. I mean, I couldn't even step onto a spelling-bee stage at a county fair.

I know the truth about approval ratings. I really do. The passages are underlined in my Bible, reminding me that seeking the approval of people is completely overrated—and entirely sinful. In the hall closet, Bible study workbooks bear witness to my penned promises to change, *once and for all.*

In 2005, under Beth Moore's tutelage, I wrote in a workbook, "I want to live for an Audience of One."

In 2006: "I need to stop seeking the approval of others and seek first the approval of God!"

In 2009: "What is at the root here? For me, the approval of others."

Beth Moore, do you have a course designed for women with skulls as thick as mine—and skin as thin as mine?

I think of my friend Jessica, a thirty-one-year-old farmer's wife in Oregon, who recently confessed her own struggle with approval and insecurity. Her admission surprised me. Jessica is the portrait of all-togetherness. She's jaw-droppingly beautiful with a gorgeous smile, a sunny personality, and adorable boys. But under that Rapunzel-like mane, she also suffers from Thick Skull Syndrome.

"Oh yeah. I've had faith in what the Bible says. *For others.* I have believed it for *them*—that God loves them, just as they are, right where they are," Jessica said.

But at times, Jessica can't believe God's truth for herself. So she has looked for love and approval from the people in her life. "I feel like every decision I make—even dinner!— must be validated by others, like I need a stamp of approval. And if I *am* complimented, I justify it away."

Trish and I are thinking of inviting her to that flagship AAA club we've been joking about, because Jessica wants what we want. And we want to say good-bye to the approval-o-meters. We're ready to say, "So long, insecurity!"

And, by golly, Beth Moore did write that book after all. In *So Long, Insecurity*, Beth says, "We're going to have to let truth scream louder to our souls than the lies that have infected us."[1]

Jessica and I are with you, Beth Moore. We want truth to scream louder than the distorted love language of that bossy, insistent idol standing between us and God.

I confess that I have been a slow learner. And my efforts to embrace the truth have felt so futile sometimes, like trying to convince myself that—with enough effort—I could pole-vault over a barn.

But lately, I have felt my Christ identity burning under my ribs, searing the edges of the Love Idol by the power of a holy flame. As a mother, I want to lead by example. How many times have the girls seen me suck in my post-baby gut, scowl at my reflection, run away from the camera, or fret over the way our house looks before guests arrive? How often have my children witnessed me shaking my head in disbelief, just like Jessica, when someone pays me a compliment? If you're a mother, you know how parenting lays bare the heart of a human being. We ache for a different way for our children. If we can't muster up the courage to change for our own good, maybe we can change for them. We want to set an example, to end any generational curses, and to pioneer a better way Home.

I think about all of that now, as I tug at the blankets with tense fists. Memorized Scripture tumbles out of my mouth:

> Am I now trying to win the approval of men, or of God? Or am I trying to please men? If I were still trying to please men, I would not be a servant of Christ. (Galatians 1:10, NIV)

I want to smash that Love Idol to smithereens. Maybe if a person preaches from the self-pulpit enough, she can magically flip an interior switch. I want to believe it will be different this time.

But what would real, committed change require? How do I declare war on my own heart?

I grit my teeth and hurl whispered hope into the darkness of my bedroom: "It *will* be different. It will. Right, Lord?" I roll over, pulling my pillow over my ear, hoping to muffle any lies that might come bouncing back.

The digital numbers on the clock blur, so I grope for

my glasses on the nightstand. It's 5:30. Half of my queen-size bed is empty. My husband slipped out the door thirty minutes ago to begin his farm chores in the coolness of morning.

I stare into a dark corner. And I wait for light.

I remember again how, in the sixth grade, I proclaimed with certainty and conviction that I would one day write books: "I *will* be an author."

Yes, that's what I wrote.

But I haven't spoken those words aloud since I was twelve. The notion of a book never really disappeared. I simply shoehorned it into a hiding spot between my fear and my pride. That's the modus operandi of the approval-seeking perfectionist: Her dreams are kept secret. That way, if I do try something ridiculously brave—like writing a book—but then fail, no one will know the difference. *If* I try . . .

If.

Madeleine L'Engle's words whisper down through the decades, to reach me here, where I'm curved in a cocoon of bedcovers: "If I thought I had to say it better than anybody else, I'd never start."[2]

But, Madeleine, you were another kind of woman, I think. A better, braver kind. What do you say to a woman like Jennifer, a modern-day Much-Afraid?

Madeleine answers, again in old words: "Only a fool is not afraid."[3]

Where can a woman find the courage to try something—for heaven's sake, for the sake of really living—without worrying how it will affect people's opinion of her? We know the theological answer, and it's on the tips of our tongues: "I can do everything through Christ, who gives me strength" (Philippians 4:13). But there is a difference between having Scripture memorized and knowing it "by heart." I want my heart to know, so my heart can really live.

Sometimes friends would ask if I'd ever try to write a book, now that I was done with my years of newspapering. They know I teach writing at Dordt College. And some knew I had started a faith blog after a long writing hiatus. The blog was a writing venture that I would consider uncharacteristically brave of my fear-filled self. Until 2008, I had rarely written any stories about my own life. I preferred asking others the tough questions. The notepad and tape recorder were shields that gave me safe hiding places.

When friends would ask if a book were coming, I would crinkle my nose. "Nah. I don't have any real interest in that sort of thing."

If they would ask why, I'd tell them I prefer the short-term gratification that comes from five-hundred-word blog posts. I'd cross my arms over my chest, turn down the corners of my mouth, then tell them that I didn't have the stomach for the demands of the publishing industry.

But that wasn't true. What I didn't have a stomach for was this: rejection, which is a symptom of this long-standing showdown with validation. I feared the potential rejection of

publishers who might not like my style. And if a publisher
were interested, I feared the rejection of readers. I really *did*
have a book waiting to be written. I felt I had a message that
would resonate with other women. God had been working it
out in me, and He'd been nudging me for months. But I had
stuffed it away, afraid of rejection.

It's crazy. I mean, I have a deep and passionate love for
a Savior who rescued me from the deepest pits of doubt.
I am brought to tears regularly by my Savior's grace, which
saved a wretch like me. But the old nature still haunts me,
linking arms with the enemy. Even believers can get sucked
into this vortex of anxiety.

We can be sealed for eternity, Christ-bought and heaven-
bound, but still live like cowards, locked down by the chains
of what people might think of us. We can live out of our
need for a *reputation*, rather than our promise of *redemption*.

I wonder how many Kingdom dreams have died at the
feet of the enemy, who convinces people that their work
might be criticized or rejected.

Fear has a way of carrying God-planted dreams into dark
corners, while the Accuser hisses a single, debilitating word:
Coward. Heart thumping, you remember how you've failed
before. You remind yourself of false starts. Fearful of repeated
failure, you tame your marvelously delicious dreams. After a
while, you forget that you had those dreams in the first place.
You coax them into submission, until they become slippery
mirages. And then eventually, your dreams slink away, dis-
appearing behind the baseboards of your bedroom wall.

They are nothing anymore. And no one will know the difference. Because you never told. And you never tried.

On humid Iowa mornings, Scott leaves early to tend to the pigs and crops. The old, blue Ford rumbles down the country lane, kicking up dust as it follows a well-worn path toward the pig barns. I reach my hand over to his side of the bed, to run my palm along the empty, wrinkled space beside me. He has slept next to me for fifteen years. I call him my "God's Got It" guy.

"God's Got It." That is his repeated mantra on the farm, because he can't control the weather or the markets. And his philosophy for farming has become a way of seeing the world. In those three words, my man encapsulates his entire theology. These words, he says, deliver him from the worry that sprouts from the unpredictable nature of living on planet Earth. He says it's the only way he can make sense of anything at all, in a world replete with wild uncertainty. This farmer's words have begun to cut a groove in me. And I've begun to repeat them too. Because I know this: What we say to ourselves, and to one another, can determine whether we live imprisoned or free.

If he's the "God's Got It" guy, I have too often been the "God, Prove It" girl. I have a track record of distrusting my Maker. Even after God granted me a saving faith, I have been such a Thomas, wanting to put my hands into the wound in Jesus' side. I am fairly certain, from personal experience, that there is such a thing as faith smaller than a mustard seed (see Matthew 17:20).

When I was in college, my journalism professors demanded accuracy. They even offered us this bit of advice: "If your mother says she loves you, double-check it." That was great advice for a news reporter, but disastrous when applied to a faith walk. If God says He loves you, do you double-check that too?

The mantra "God's Got It" had once felt risky at best, perhaps even dangerous, because it placed all the control in the hands of an unseen Being. But the more I have seen and felt God at work in my own life, the more I have begun to believe that He does, indeed, have it.

When I confessed my doubts about writing this book, my "God's Got It" guy knew that a yet-to-be-written manuscript had stuck its foot in the door of my heart, asking to be penned. He was married to its alleged author, and together, he and I had experienced the freedom of loosed chains. But he also knew that sometimes his wife was still oversensitive to the opinions of others. He was keenly aware that, in theory, this book would help women understand that they are loved and adored by the Savior, regardless of their approval rating. Furthermore, he knew that the biggest obstacle in front of this book wasn't the publishing industry. The biggest obstacle was his wife. She hadn't penned a single word of the book, and already she was asking the question: What if they don't approve?

And what if they do? I can look back and see the

pitfalls of responding to cultural barometers of popularity and accomplishment. I know the jarring truth from first-hand experience: Worldly success can deliver far more destructive blows to the spiritual self than worldly failure can. Believers can fashion little-g gods out of their big-G God-gifts. I remember how intoxicating those bylines were, years earlier. What if the book became an idol?

"You've married a woman of paradox," I tell Scott one morning, shaking my head. On the verge of tears, I explain that "I feel like I'm jumping into a pit of my worst fears."

Scott adjusts his farmer's cap, and he laughs. *He laughs!* He says he's not making fun of me. He tosses his work-worn hands into the air, giddy and with eyes afire. I see that he is believing *for* me, like a disciple who sprints into the room to tell Thomas: "We have seen the Lord!" (John 20:25).

"Maybe that's the point!" my husband says, pressing his fist into his palm. "Maybe jumping into your fear is the point. That's why they call it courage."

I cross my arms over my chest, cock my head, and give him "the look." I demand proof before I jump. I don't walk tightropes without first checking the pins on the safety net.

I know I'm not alone. Friends tell me they're scared too. Scared to apply for a promotion at work, start a business, speak in public, pray out loud, enroll in a class. So many of us look in the mirror and see only the flaws. We view ourselves as too stumbling and bumbling, too broken or clueless or sinful to be effective. We think we're unremarkable, so we run from the Kingdom challenges placed before us.

"Jennifer," my husband coaxes, "just *enjoy* it. Tell your story. Tell any story. Just write. Throw your words into the world."

He puts an arm around my waist, pulls me in, and whispers his three favorite words: "God's got it."

With a half smile, I retort: "Maybe *you* should write the book."

I lean my head on his chest, hoping farmer-faith like his can be attained through osmosis.

Is such a faith formed when your will has no choice but to bend? How can I get faith like that—the kind that is sure of what I hope for and certain of what I do not see?[4] My husband can scratch back the dirt and drop tiny pearls from the planter, but he can't make the skies open. He can tug open stitched bags of designer seeds, but he can't cajole a green shoot from a pod. He can use GPS technology, but he can't prevent a hailstorm. He can mouse-click his way through forecasts all he wants to, but a snowstorm can still whip through his fields before the harvest ends. Does he have any choice, other than "God's Got It"?

I suppose he does have choices. We all have two choices in times of angst or worry: raise the fist or bend the will.

I think of Jesus, agonizing in the garden of Gethsemane, hours before the sin of all humanity crushed into His forehead, His feet, and His wrists. Jesus—fully man, but also fully God—could have raised His fist under the canopy of olive trees. It brings me to tears thinking of it, how the Savior bowed lower and lower for us. Christ stooped low enough for someone to pound iron spikes into His flesh, then endured death of the most slow and painful kind—excruciating, in fact. That word, *excruciating*, means in Latin "out of crucifying." And yet Christ spoke these words the night before, in the quiet of the trees: "Not my will, but yours be done" (Luke 22:42, NIV).

I watch, time and again, how my man's humility resembles his Savior's. Through his daily sacrifices, I see how my husband bends his will toward a God who's "got it" and who is in the process of "getting" me. I can feel it.

I turn in the bed, toward the window.

Morning's first light has painted a faded pink line behind the curved row of spruce trees out back. Dust cakes the single window overlooking the backyard from our bedroom. I've never washed that window because no one else ever sees it. That's what I do, see? I let the unseen window stay dirty but keep the front ones sparkly clean. A Pharisee's guide to window cleaning, I think.

I reach for my Bible on the nightstand and unzip the leather cover.

I wonder again, *What will real change require?* It will take more than memorized words. I need a soul-deep work—not just so I might write a book someday. This isn't about a book or a writing career. Is it ever about just one thing? There's more at stake here. I need a cleansing of interior windows.

I don't need to write my own words in a book. I need to allow God to write better words on my life.

The weight of God's Word feels heavy on my outstretched legs. I find Paul's story in the book of Acts. Hortense Cochrane taught me this story as a child, in the basement of the Methodist church where little wooden chairs formed a crescent by the piano. I am in need of relearning old Sunday school lessons.

I leaf through pages, finding snippets of the apostle's biography, pre-Jesus. My forefinger traces Paul's impressive list of achievements: chief cheerleader of traditional religion, later promoted to team captain; a top-notch education; a sharp mind; a pedigree bloodline; a rock-star résumé. He was the envy of his peers, the shining jewel in his teacher's crown.

And right here, in Acts . . . a story about the king of credentials, standing in the wings at an execution. Men with stones in their fists ask Paul—then called Saul—if he would mind watching their coats while they pelt Stephen with rocks. "And Saul approved of their killing him" (Acts 8:1, NIV).

Saul was a perfectionist on a frenzied path toward . . . what? Where does such feverish, intense living lead a person? I flip forward two pages. Outside, the sun rises higher, chasing the last bits of darkness. In this bedroom, more shadows skitter away.

Suddenly a light from heaven flashed around him.
He fell to the ground. (Acts 9:3-4, NIV)

Jesus speaks.

And I am dropped to the ground, next to Saul on the road to Damascus.

Sometimes a face-plant into the dirt is the best way to humble the hurried and the harried. One of Judaism's best and brightest has to be led by the hand, just so he can get to his destination. I follow them into Damascus. For the next three days, Saul can't see. He can't eat or drink. Then in one magical moment, he regains his sight when something like scales fall from his eyes. Someone baptizes him. He eats dinner. And life as he knew it changes.

I pick up *The Message* paraphrase of the Bible, comparing texts. I flip pages from Acts to Philippians. From Saul to Paul. I come across the memorable passage in which Paul compares his credentials to "dog dung" (Philippians 3:8, *The Message*).

I lift my eyes from these words and stare forward, catching my reflection in the dresser mirror. On the other side of the house, old nails pin my decade-old newspaper-writing awards to the wall. Small idols, gathering dust.

I drop my gaze to the page again. To Paul, a first-class résumé and diploma were suddenly better suited for birdcage lining than brassy frames. "I consider everything a loss," he proclaims (Philippians 3:8, NIV).

Paul writes to the Galatians and to the Corinthians, and he writes also to the Midwestern farmer's wife. The repeated refrain of Paul, a kindred spirit, cuts deep: Stop chasing the approval of people.

But was Paul an approval seeker like me? Did he crave validation, or was he merely working "heartily, as to the Lord" (Colossians 3:23, NKJV)? I go searching, returning to the words that I had highlighted in green years earlier: "If I were still trying to please people, . . ." he writes (Galatians 1:10, NIV).

Still.

That one word. *Still.*

Is this a hint at a former internal struggle in the life of a changed man? I do know that it was important enough to Paul that he thought it worth mentioning over and over again.

He speaks to the Romans about approval from God, instead of men: "A person with a changed heart seeks praise from God, not from people" (2:29).

To the people of Corinth, he writes, "'Let the one who boasts boast in the Lord.' For it is not the one who commends himself who is approved, but the one whom the Lord commends" (2 Corinthians 10:17-18, NIV).

And for the people of Thessalonica, he says, "We are not trying to please people but God, who tests our hearts" (1 Thessalonians 2:4, NIV).

Those are the words of a man who apparently had once warmed himself under the glowing praise of people. Those are the words of a man with a changed heart and a singular, refreshed purpose. If Jesus can change Paul, Jesus can change the rest of us. Paul's conversion story is a "God's Got It" story.

I bow my head over old words, looking again and again at what God can do, letting theological truth burrow into my soul.

Jesus spoke. Jesus commanded. The Lord told. The Holy Spirit filled. And by whose power did the scales fall? God's.

The active subject here is the Lord, not Paul. Not you, nor I. But God.

God did. God does. God will. God's will.

God's got it.

I pray it then, with tears burning my eyes: "God, You've got it. Please, get *me*. Save me from myself. And keep saving me. Smash the Love Idol, and let Your love set me free to be who You made me to be."

We want this, don't we? We want an emancipated heart, free from the bondage of self-concern. Maybe you're like me: You've been saved by grace, have repented repeatedly, have been forgiven seventy-times-seven times. You've said the creeds and the prayers and have walked to the altar again and again. You've memorized verse upon verse and raised your hands and your voice in the sanctuary. You may be a Bible study leader, a church volunteer, a committed believer with a heart burning within you (see Luke 24:32).

Yet this: you, like me, ache. We are freed women, aching. We want to become more like our Savior.

And so early this morning, as the apostle Paul's words echo in my ears, I realize that my Love Idols have lost their sheen. I am so done with the earthly accolades. I want the "divine accolade" of Christ.[5] Just give me Jesus. I know it, as sure as I can taste the salt in these tears: After years of doing what the Love Idol required of me, I want to sever that unhealthy relationship.

I pray to God, right here under the covers. I open my laptop and tap out words, pouring them all out like water from a faucet. Words tumble out of me in waves, like a flood, a confession:

Dear God,

I'm such a two-faced spiritual klutz. I'm saved, but I stumble. I'm a sinner, made a saint. I am, indeed, the wretch the song refers to.

But You, God? You've loved me anyway. Even before I thought to love You back, You loved me. And You still do. You've had it, and You've still "got it."

Would You keep on getting me?

You've told me that mirrors are poor judges. A person can look in the mirror or the inbox or the bank account or the offering plate, and if things look good, life is good. And if things look bleak, well . . . life seems bleak. I heard You say it loud under my very own skin: Stop. Looking. In. The. Mirrors. They are horrible indicators of reality.

Yeah, mirrors reflect a false truth sometimes.

I do want to reflect You.

I've lived otherwise, at times. I've paid too much attention to mirrors—and to glitter. There's a lot of glitter in the world. And there are a thousand ways to count shiny things: followers, Facebook friends, Twitter @mentions, and invitations. But there's only One Way that ever really mattered.

Lord, help me follow that Way.

There are also a hundred ways to measure if a lowly mortal is insignificant, especially if she's been overlooked, overmatched, overburdened, overtopped. I want to be so over that.

There's always someone out there telling us we've got to have a bigger voice, a better house, more money, more influence.

You know it already, Lord, but let me say it out loud here: The world tells me to be all the things that end in y: funny, pretty, skinny, witty. I'll turn it upside down and chase after the One whose name begins with y—You, Yahweh.

You know what, Lord? I have looked in mirrors. I have. I confess that to You. But . . . that's the thing about You, Yahweh. That's the amazing thing about this still-amazing grace, Jesus. You take our chins in Your nail-scarred hands. And You pull our eyes off ourselves, daily readjusting our gaze so we're fixed on You.

I see You.

And it's so good to be seen by You.

You are the God who sees, my El Roi. And we all want to be seen, I suppose, to know that we matter.

You tell us that we do matter.

I want You to know how much that means to me.

And I think I'm only beginning to really understand it.

Thank You, Father, for being patient with Your daughter.

My bedroom door opens before I finish tapping at the keyboard. In the doorway, I see the silhouette of our younger daughter, Anna. She comes closer, rubbing her fists into her sleepy eyes. I pat my hand on her daddy's spot, and she shuffles toward the bed. I zip my Bible closed and shut my laptop. She curls beside me, all pink in a ruffly Disney princess gown. I wrap my arm around her waist, pull her in tight. I can smell last night's bath in her hair. I breathe in lavender.

I want to recalibrate my heart—for the sake of the girls and for the sake of a God-honoring life. It's true: I'm not yet who I'm made to be, for I am still becoming.

But equally true is this: I am not the woman I was.

In what ways do you suspect your Love Idol has thrust its bossy self between you and God's plans for your life?

CHAPTER 7

"DO YOU WANT TO GET WELL?"

But the man who is not afraid to admit everything that he sees
to be wrong with himself, and yet recognizes that he may be
the object of God's love precisely because of his shortcomings,
can begin to be sincere. His sincerity is based on
confidence, not in his own illusions about himself,
but in the endless, unfailing mercy of God.

THOMAS MERTON

MY IPHONE BEEPS WHILE I sit with Anna in a waiting room thick with the scent of antiseptic.

It's Chris, a dear friend of ours who is a pastor.

Earlier in the day, I had e-mailed a few friends, asking for prayers. I told them I was writing a book, stepping straight into my fear, regardless of rejection. It felt like obedience, like an act of love and trust in a God who's "got it." Chris texts me a question: "What is the book about?"

This is the day I tell him about the book I'm writing—me, a woman still seeking full freedom from the clutches of the Love Idol.

And this is the day he texts me with his answer: "The cure is the process."

He is saying that it is all right if I don't have all the answers yet, because these things take time—often a *life*time.

I scan his words, letting them do a deep work in me. Anna leans her head on my shoulder while she pages through a *Highlights* magazine.

A baby cries. A mother rubs the warm back of a flushed toddler. An ashen man with iron-gray hair and crutches sits like a mannequin across the aisle, watching a television show about an underwater sponge who wears a necktie and lives in a pineapple.

This place is crammed with the sick and injured. Like my Anna.

I've brought her here for an X-ray and a diagnosis. She has complained of foot pain for several weeks. We tried home remedies. We applied ice, then heat, then ice again. We massaged and stretched. We tried waiting it out. Nothing worked. We have struggled against an unnamed pain. We need a name, a cure.

And now, while I sit waiting for a physical diagnosis for Anna, this pastor is texting me with a *spiritual* diagnosis. *For me.* He calls the cure "the process."

Huh.

Maybe you're like me. Maybe you have not always been into process. Maybe you have preferred the quick fix, the promise of three steps to a better you. Or better yet, a full-blown miracle. *Poof.* We're fixed! God could do that if He wanted to, but I'm getting the idea that He has something more to teach us, right in the middle of our battle.

I know enough about life as a human being to know this: The walk of a believer is not a drive-through service. Faith is not microwavable.

Maybe part of the journey is admitting we've got a problem. Just the other day, I flipped through my Beth Moore workbooks, and this time, I found these notes on page 147 of *Breaking Free*. I was startled by my bluntness. "I suffer from bondage to the obstacle of approval and pride because I haven't yielded to God's authority in that area."

If nothing else, at least I was honest. It has taken another few years for my heart to get the memo that my brain wrote. I knew the problem, but I wasn't serious about moving on.

I confess: I'm *still* not all that interested in admitting my struggle publicly. Who wants to expose the unflattering truth that something is broken on the inside?

Admitting your weakness is the time-tested, single-most-important first step for anyone seeking a cure. Mothers of feverish babies call pediatricians. Recovering alcoholics admit they have a problem over which they are powerless. In the Bible, a woman who has been bleeding for twelve years straight reaches a hand out to Jesus. She hopes to steal a cure from the hem of the Nazarene's garment. Jesus could have quietly cured the woman, then walked away. But no. Jesus stops in the middle of the crowd, turns, and asks a question that He already knows the answer to: "Who touched me?"

Cringing in the crowd, the woman admits her deepest

need for a cure. Those words are underlined in my Bible. "Then the woman, seeing that she could not go unnoticed, came trembling and fell at his feet. In the presence of all the people, *she told why she had touched him*" (Luke 8:47, NIV, emphasis mine).

She told. She admitted. She fessed up.

What was true two thousand years ago is still true today: To be cured of anything, a patient must first admit her need. Could we do that? Right here, in front of God and everybody? Could we, trembling, fall at His feet?

Here in the waiting room, half a dozen people wear their sickness on the outside; they slump, hack, whimper. They've come for help, admitting need. That is always step one.

I sit among the ailing. I am aware, however, that I am in my own way afflicted with a disease—a spiritual one that Scripture pinpoints repeatedly.

Before any cure comes the diagnosis.

Am I ready for a diagnosis of the soul and the hard road that might follow?

For years I have clung to my need for validation, clutching it to my chest like a favorite stuffed teddy bear. I hide behind my smile and polished exterior. My house isn't spit-shined, but if you're coming over for a visit, I'll make you *think* it is. I'm the person who wants to have the right answers, the right clothes, the A grade, even though no one is handing out report cards to farmwives.

Yes, to get better, I *will* need a diagnosis. But do I really want a cure?

❦

If I'm completely honest, I have liked my sickness at times.

It's been a steady companion since kindergarten. I remember now how I sat in my classroom one afternoon, unable to figure out a problem on a math worksheet. I kept writing and erasing, writing and erasing—until I tore a rippled hole in the paper. I handed in the worksheet to my teacher, pushing it slowly across the lacquered wooden top of her desk. She frowned when she glanced at the paper. I couldn't get the problem right, so she thrust the paper back at me, again and again.

With each wrong answer, the teacher's frown deepened. She scolded me with a wrinkled, wagging finger. How could I miss a simple math problem? And how could I *keep* getting it wrong when all my classmates knew the right answer? She motioned to the other kindergartners, zipping up their winter coats for recess. I would be required to stay at my desk until I came up with the correct answer. Fat tears plopped on my worksheet. I wiped my nose with the back of my hand. I scribbled answers with a stubby pencil until I stumbled upon the solution. And when I got it right, it was only because I guessed.

When I handed her my paper the last time, she smiled at my happy accident. She stamped a red smiley face on the page.

The message:

Success = smiley face.

Right answer = full acceptance.

Her approval was more important to me than knowing how I arrived at the right answer—more important, even, than recess.

That is my first memory of the false sense of security that comes with someone's stamp of approval. In kindergarten, that stamp came quite literally, with a smudged smiley face in the right-hand corner of a worksheet.

I felt like I had been rescued from sea and pulled ashore onto a small island where I could rest for a while. But then, more waves of insecurity would break against the shore, pulling me back out to sea.

Lorretta, a writer friend of mine in Georgia, told me the other day that she rode those same waves. But as a child, she could rarely find the little islands of respite. She sought the love of an abusive stepmother. "The only way I could avoid her wrath was to clean house," Lorretta told me. "Nobody will hurt you if you are busy scrubbing the floors and toilets."

One Mother's Day, little Lorretta labored over some magazines with construction paper and glue. She made her stepmom a card with the words "I love you, Mom," hoping the gift would keep her safe on one of those happy little islands.

It worked . . . but only for a few days.

She soon found herself out in the waves again, looking for someone's love to keep her afloat.

Those early days shaped Lorretta's understanding of her world and herself. When she grew up, she sought love and acceptance from everyone in her life.

She wanted her Love Idol to be a life preserver, but it nearly took her under instead.

Until Jesus.

I've lived almost four decades treading water between islands and tidal waves. I've been buoyed by praise, rescued by recognition, deflated by criticism—even in the church. I've said it before, but it bears repeating: It's okay to receive affirmation. It's fine to offer praise or compliments. And it's vital to our spiritual well-being to receive the love of others. We were designed by God to love and be loved. But we have to ask ourselves, how often have we twisted love into an idol? How often do we identify our worth according to the love and approval of others? If we're starting to drown, do we hope that someone will toss us a ring of validation to hang on to? Or do we, like Lorretta, reach out for Jesus instead?

I understand, it can be hard to imagine a life in which we don't care what people think anymore, especially when our brains have been trained for years to seek their approval. We've drifted through life this way for years. Without our little arm floaties, won't we drown?

God is calling us to His arms instead—where we receive *His* approval and acceptance. Jesus' words to the religious leaders in John 5 are also for us. They are hard words to hear: "How can you believe if you accept praise from one another, yet make no effort to obtain the praise that comes from the only God?" (John 5:44, NIV).

The Beatitudes say that the humble will inherit the earth. Humility is a finicky thing, always hiding as soon as it's identified. But I do know that humility might involve admitting one's own weakness, perhaps even publicly. So maybe this would be a good first step, to blurt out my misguided worship with these words, right here:

"Hi, my name is Jennifer Dukes Lee. And I've been a Love Idol worshiper."

A nurse carrying a clipboard scans the waiting room.

"Anna Lee?"

My daughter and I follow the woman to the X-ray room. Anna limps, and I hold her hand.

Anna climbs onto the X-ray table. The nurse instructs her to hold her legs straight out with her feet flexed. Anna knows how this works. A few years ago, we came here after we couldn't find a missing blue marble from a Discovery Toys game. Anna later confessed that she "wanted to see what it tasted like." Sure enough, the X-ray technician found the marble, pointing on the computer screen to a perfect dot under Anna's rib cage. Even my untrained eye could identify a swallowed marble on an X-ray.

This time, it's different. I don't really know what we're looking for. The X-ray machine shoots out invisible beams, capturing an image. I watch the computer screen from behind the wall, with my arms folded across my chest. I see my daughter's bones appear digitally on the screen. My eyes strain to make out anything unusual. And then: *Aha, right there.*

The technician clicks her computer mouse, and the picture disappears. But I have already seen it. What was that bump? I saw it on the heel of Anna's foot. I know what a swallowed marble looks like, but this? It was a long, thick . . . something.

"Can I see the X-ray again, please?" I ask. I suck in my breath, holding it deep in my lungs, as the technician brings the picture up on the screen. I let my air out in one short burst.

"Here," I say, tapping the digital image with my forefinger. "That doesn't look right."

The technician stands up from her swivel chair, purses her lips, shakes her head. She's not allowed to tell me what she sees. "The doctor will have the results ready for you in a few minutes."

Anna and I retrace our steps down the hallways, back to the waiting room. I turn on my iPhone again, Googling for answers.

I punch in the search terms on a tiny keyboard with my thick, clumsy thumbs: "Growth on child's heel."

The Internet search produces 2.34 million possibilities. But before I have time to click on even one link, the nurse calls us to the examination room, where a sign says, "Please turn off cell phones."

✧

Sometimes, all you really want is a name. And even Google can't help.

The white paper under Anna crinkles as she fidgets. We talk about the pretty paintings on the wall. We discuss where we will eat afterward. I smile a fake smile. Conversation masks a mom's worry, but worst-case scenarios multiply like cancer cells.

I fight back fear with a reality check: I mean, do I *really* think she'll be diagnosed with a foot tumor? That's not likely.

But I need a name. We need names for the problems that haunt us. Naming precedes the cure.

The doctor knocks, then opens the door. She names the disease, even before she introduces herself. "What we've got here is Sever's disease. Apophysitis," she says, flopping Anna's medical charts on the counter by the sink basin. She writes the diagnosis on a scrap of paper and hands it to me.

"It's a common cause of heel pain among kids her age. She'll grow out of it." The doctor's cheery warmth spills over the room. I unclench my balled fists.

"And the bump I saw on the X-ray? What was that?" I ask her. She tells me that the bump is a growth plate. There's nothing weird growing on my daughter's foot. I sigh my relief.

The doctor says Anna will need inserts in her shoes, ice, and ibuprofen. No jump rope or hopscotch for two weeks. Healing takes time, the doctor says.

The doctor tells us the disease will resurface on and off over the next few years until Anna's done growing. But with a name, we know what it is, and we know how to respond if the pain flares up again.

This will take time. Ah yes, some cures take time. Even

illnesses that once seemed cured have a way of resurfacing. "Until we're done growing . . ."

I'll need to remember this. For Anna, the cure will be in the process. I feel the weight of my cell phone in my pocket, with wise words stored in a text message.

I, too, will need to consult a professional. I won't find my answers on Google, but in God.

~∿∾~

On a late summer morning, my cure-in-process begins to find its voice. I hear it speaking just after the day's first golden rays spill onto my pine kitchen table. I sit with a steaming cup of coffee and my Bible, watching the sun rise over the waving cornfields. I unzip the leather cover, and the Bible falls open to a story of healing in John 5. Maybe you could call this my holy prescription, an unexpected Rx for the soul, a holy house call from the Great Physician. Some people call these sorts of things coincidences. But I've come to know them as God-incidences. These are moments when the Lord's providence leaps out at you, somewhat unexpectedly.

Sure, I had read the story in John 5 before. But there's reading, and then there's *reading*. Today, I find myself *reading*. I adjust my glasses.

This is the story of a sick man in need of a cure. The Bible says he was "an invalid for thirty-eight years" (v. 5, NIV) who came to a healing pool in Jerusalem every day. Each morning, he found himself in that same spot, among the blind, the lame, and the paralyzed. All of them waited poolside for a cure.

When I had previously read about that man by the pool, I shook my head, thinking to myself, *Poor old sap.*

But on this day, with the pages opened heavenward, I lift my head and stare at the kitchen wall. I widen my eyes and say the words out loud: "I am that poor old sap by the healing pool. That's me!"

I scan the story again. Then again—this time more slowly. And I drop myself into it, landing right by the pool.

I'm the "invalid," hanging out among the ailing who wait for a cure. I can feel the cool, hard stone through my cloak. The early-morning chill blowing against my back is the only proof I'm still alive. Most days, people walk around me or step over me, like I'm a half-dead dog. And they're probably half-right.

Today, the city is crammed full of people. I hear the buzz of excitement. Feet shuffle past my head. The high-pitched laughter of reunited friends echoes through the courtyard. They've come to Jerusalem for a feast. But while they party, I pout. I figure my day will begin and end the same way it always has: marking long hours by watching shadows fall over covered colonnades.

I look around and see the usuals here. I know them by their ailments and the sound of their pained moans. But, as far as I know, no one has been here as long as I have. I've been coming here to a pool called Bethesda for nearly forty years, stretching out on my smelly, old mat.

I'm waiting for a miracle.

I've seen it happen from time to time. A mysterious hand agitates the water in the pool. Some folks say it's an angel of the Lord. The first one to touch the stirred waters always walks away with the prize: a cure. But me? I can never get there fast enough. And if I'm being honest, I'm not sure I want a cure anyway. My illness has become a way of life, a steady companion. Some days I feel trapped by my sickness; other days—crazy as it sounds to some— I can't imagine life without it.

I don't know it yet, but this day will be different. In a life with few choices, I'll finally get one.

I overhear someone say that a man from Nazareth has come into town through the Sheep Gate, the entrance usually reserved for Temple-sacrifice animals. He calls Himself the Good Shepherd. His sandals slap on the ground as He inches closer. And suddenly, He's standing beside me, close enough for me to touch. I see His dusty toes. I turn my head upward to look at Him, silhouetted against the sky. I shield my eyes; He bends a knee. We're eye-to-eye now. I can tell by the way He's looking at me that He knows me better than I know myself. He even knows how long I've been here. Turns out, I started coming to this place even before this fellow was born on a starry night in Bethlehem.

The Good Shepherd has a question: "Do you want to get well?"

I don't give Him a direct answer. I'm good at diversions and disguises.

"Sir," I say, "I have no one to help me into the pool when the water is stirred. While I am trying to get in, someone else goes down ahead of me."

And then the Good Shepherd makes a demand: "Get up! Pick up your mat and walk."

I could stay, stretched out by a familiar pool, on a familiar mat, among familiar friends. This has been my life for thirty-eight years. What if I try to stand, but my knees give out? What if I stand, but I can't walk? What if I start walking, but I fall?

And what if I miss the strange comfort of my ailment?

But I do it. I stand anyway, unfolding my body, one vertebra at a time until I am vertical. I notice how my shadow appears upright for the first time in decades, and right next to my shadow, I see this: the shadow of the One who healed me.

And then, only then, do I have the guts to take my first step.

I mark the words of the story with my green highlighter. But can I live those words? Can I live what I believe? How do I take these brain-deep answers and make them heart-deep?

I take a sip of coffee and set down my mug. I read the study notes in my Bible, which suggest that sick people can develop a peculiar fondness for their illnesses. "After 38 years, this man's problem had become a way of life. . . . He had no hope of ever being healed and no desire to help himself. The man's situation looked hopeless."[1]

Until Jesus walked in.

I have stretched out by my own Bethesda daily, waiting for the waters of approval to stir, and wondering, *What is wrong with me?*

Why do we live in this cycle of validation, swept up by the empty promises of the Love Idol, only to sink down when someone rejects us? We make frenetic jumps from island to island between tidal waves of insecurity. Beth Moore says culture has "thrown us under the bus. We have a fissure down the spine of our souls."[2] We want to keep up appearances. We want to avoid criticism. We treat our lives like a stat sheet, trying to keep score the world's way.

I'm sad for all the ways man's opinion has become more important than God's approval.

And I am tired of it.

I scan the story in the Gospel of John. How many years? I make a note of it, scribbling it in the margin: "38 years." Thirty-eight!

The lump in my throat swells as I note the similarity. I am thirty-nine. I have been chained to my smelly mat of validation, next to a magic pool of approval, for thirty-nine years.

My eyes flutter shut to pray. "Dear God, please . . . help." I don't know what else to say. So I just sit, hunched over this polished pine rectangle, with yesterday's Cheerios under my bare toes. And I listen.

In times like these, with my spirit stilled, I can hear the sandaled feet of the Good Shepherd coming my way.

And this morning, I already know what He's going to ask me. He's going to make me answer the question He asked the man by the pool: *Do you want to get well?*

I know that I will enter into full healing only if I answer yes, then stand upright.

I keep my eyes cinched closed. Here He comes, slower now. What will it be? *Do you want to get well?*

God-power resides here, in this place where the naming meets the nemesis, where the Light meets the dark. This is perhaps why lives change in rooms with closed doors, where famous first words are uttered quietly into a circle of understanding faces: "Hi, my name is [insert name here]. And I am an [insert addiction here]."

We know it's true: To let go of something, you have to first admit you're holding on to it. The moment you're willing to call the problem by its actual name, you're one step closer to canceling its power over you.

The Good Shepherd is here, having passed through the Sheep Gate. He whispers the question, *Do you want to get well?* But it feels like a shout.

Twenty-seven years after Mrs. Huseman named the problem, I might, at last, be ready. After years of living with a farmer who tells me, "God's got it," maybe I'm willing to live like I believe that. Not only for my children, but for the sake of a God who loves me just because He loves me.

I suck in my breath, like a pilgrim who is surprised that she's caught a glimpse of the right way home. But no one is forcing me to follow the Way. I do have choices: I can say yes to Christ or yes to my self-manufactured approval rating. If I am really going to live up to my Savior-bought righteousness, I will begin to measure my worth not by my success but by the incalculable value of my salvation.

"The man who is elated by success and is cast down by failure is still a carnal man," writes the theologian A. W. Tozer. "At best his fruit will have a worm in it."[3]

I could go to my grave a carnal woman, dying a gradual death just inches from a magic pool, bobbing between waves and happy little islands of validation while the Love Idol quietly sinks me. Or I could arise to the voice of the Good Shepherd.

I push back my chair, and it thunders against the wood planks of my kitchen floor. I think I taste it now—the sweetness of freedom finally coming.

And right there, half a world away from the pool in Jerusalem, I loosen my fingers from the edge of the chair. I answer the Good Shepherd by straightening my back, one vertebra at a time, then putting all the weight on my heels to make my first move.

I stand.

How might naming your Love Idol bring you closer to diminishing the power it holds over you?

CHAPTER 8

PREAPPROVED

He'll validate your life in the clear light of day and
stamp you with approval at high noon.
PSALM 37:6, *The Message*

IT'S SPRING—the season of perennial hope, when winter-
weary farmers pull cultivators behind their tractors, turning
over the soil before planting. I feel a turning inside of me
too. My soul is being cultivated, like soil, by holy hands.

On the pink edge of dawn outside our open bedroom
window, a duet of robins wakes me. I lie curled in a ball
under the covers. Before I stand on my own two feet,
I need to stand up tall on the inside.

Seasons have passed since I stood in response to the call
of Christ at my own Bethesda, when He asked me, "Do you
want to get well?" Left to my own devices, I would have a
tendency to drag my error-prone self back to the "healing
pool" where I had languished for thirty-nine years.

My default response is to return to the sin that made me lovesick. So I need daily injections of gospel truth to immunize my flawed humanity. Instead of returning to Bethesda, I preach the gospel to myself every day before I rise.[1] My comforter wraps around me like a prayer shawl. "Dear God, help me get over myself today."

Getting over myself is the only way of getting more into God. It really is like John the Baptist said: "He must become greater and greater, and I must become less and less" (John 3:30). The baptizer teaches us gospel math, the arithmetic of the wisest saints.

My morning preaching-to-the-self is a way to daily "become less and less" before I put a single toe to the carpet. My prayer regimen is a small act of surrender, a practical way to deliberately pull my gaze from myself to my Savior—a lesson I learned years earlier on long car rides to news assignments but have now begun to put into daily practice. Eyes cannot look in two different directions. I want mine on Jesus—not on yesterday's failures or successes, not on today's agenda, and definitely not on the world's scorecards.

Eyes. On. Jesus.

Before we stand vertically, we must *think and see* vertically. This is the sinner's only hope for defeating any idol that stands between her soul and her fullest life. We can focus the soul's eyes upward toward Christ's face or outward toward the cultural race. The world woos, offering substitute saviors and a steady stream of temptations. Even longtime

Christians are not immune to the lure of idols, especially when these idols are dressed in creative disguises.

Because we are human, we often respond to the mega-phone of this culture in places like grocery-store checkouts, where we are subjected to endless magazine covers, each a painful reminder of some way we fall short: with our weight, our garden plot, even our Thanksgiving turkey. The world is quick to offer "three easy ways to become a better you."

I know a better Way.

Before I stand up, I pray. I return to my first love.

For I want to get well.

And I am. I am getting well.

I walk to the kitchen, pour a cup of coffee, and blink slowly at the window. A tractor pulls onto the neighbor's field in this spring ritual of turning over the earth. It is a farmer's first chance at the dirt after each winter's thaw. The prophet Ezekiel wrote of this time-honored practice nearly six hundred years before Christ was born.

Ezekiel announced that on the day the Lord cleanses Israel of its sins, "The desolate land will be cultivated instead of lying desolate in the sight of all who pass through it" (Ezekiel 36:34, NIV).

Centuries later, behold: Christ cultivated new life on the cross at Calvary with the most marvelous, scandalous act of sacrifice known to humankind.

And the Savior still cultivates people, down through two

millennia. Christ tends the fallow ground of human hearts, turning the soil over and over again so seeds can be planted. There are theological words for what happens inside of a believer as a result of the Cross—words like *justification* and *sanctification*. I am a farmer's wife, not a theologian, but looking out over these fields, I know this process must be akin to what farmers do.

I am being cultivated.

I pull a chair from the kitchen table and open my Bible, returning to the story of the man by the healing pool, that man who had been there for thirty-eight years before Christ asked him, "Do you want to get well?" The man walked away from that pool, carrying his mat along with him.

In his Gospel, John says that Jesus found that same healed man in the Temple later. And what did Jesus tell him?

My index finger runs along Jesus' words. The words are haltingly brusque: "See, you are well again. Stop sinning or something worse may happen to you" (John 5:14, NIV).

I swallow down the truth with my first sip of coffee. The command might sound alarming, almost offensive: "Stop sinning or something worse may happen to you." Jesus said *that*?

If I don't pause to look deeper, I might be inclined to slam the book shut. But I know better. I know this isn't a strong-arm tactic from the Savior. This is a form of grace. Christ offers healed sinners a kind of tough love, so that they will not stumble back to false saviors and the rancid pit of anti-gospel living. Down through the centuries, the Savior has repeatedly lifted the fallen from the holes they've dug for themselves one shovel scoop at a time.

After His grand rescue, the Redeemer does not always seal that hole shut behind us. He does not force us into relationship or bully us into repentance. Instead, He leaves us with a choice: follow Me or fall again. He invites each one of us to "pick up your mat and walk." Then Jesus reminds us to "stop sinning"—in my case, to stop worshiping the Love Idol.

The Creator of all things—including gravity—understands the physics of falling. He knows that dropping back into the deep hole we've dug for ourselves would hurt far worse than it did on the first trip down. We would tumble faster and harder into the pitch-black of our sin, unlike the slow descent that got us there over months or years.

We pray the prayer, spoken down through the centuries as taught by Christ: "Lead us not into temptation."

Sinners, saved by grace, know we need *daily* saving grace to keep us from falling. If we come to the end of ourselves, we need to stay there, for this is the sacred place where Christ's daily renewal springs forth. Christ's command to stop sinning reminds me to walk away from anti-gospel pits filled with false idols. I cling to the Savior and to the hem of His garment so I don't tip headfirst into the hole from which He pulled me.

This is one essential way: I feed on Scripture here at the kitchen table. Daily Bread nourishes. I've found food that fills—real food, not the false nourishment that comes from the Love Idol.

Closing the Bible, I shut my eyes, knowing that Christ daily calls me back to Him, my first love. I want to press in close behind the Savior.

I feel like I'm in the middle of a second conversion—the first led me toward salvation; the second, toward living like I actually believe what the Savior says. And He says He loves me. It makes me feel weak-kneed and deliriously adored.

I stood up at Christ's call, at my own Bethesda pool. But strangely, since then, I have found my soul bending ever lower. I've known for years that bowed-low humility is the way toward real relationship with God, in which we take our proper place before the King. The Good Book says that one day, every knee shall bow. But for most of my life, I was a stubborn, lock-kneed insubordinate.

When I unlocked my knees, it felt like I was falling. In love.

Steam rises from my cup, and I hold its warmth in my hands. I remind myself of gospel truth every day. That God delights in me. That I don't have to earn anyone's favor. And that the Lord who began a good work in me will carry it to completion. Paul inked those words like a promise in Philippians 1:6. Maybe it's another way of saying that the cure really is in the process, because you can't microwave spiritual growth.

We must practically preach the gospel to ourselves every day—more often as needed—to understand where we stand positionally with God. The Lord reminds me constantly that He is God; I am not. And He really needs to tell me every . . . single . . . day.

Christians are not a once-and-done people, despite what we're led to believe. The church has done a decent job of welcoming sinners, but it frowns when we don't get better quickly. Or when we fail. I know a woman, a committed follower, who was denied communion by her church's elders after a painful and public split with her husband. Another friend stopped attending her church for several months because she was an alcoholic who relapsed. She feared the judgment of others in the pews, so she avoided them altogether.

I have relapses of another kind. How many times have I barked orders at the children on Sunday mornings, snapping at them to find their Bibles and dress shoes, provoking hot tears that run down their little cheeks? We drive to church in silence, but by the time we walk in the front door, I'm wearing my polished church appearance and a smile that I'm not actually feeling on the inside. Even the most faithful churchgoers hide their faults, which sadly contributes to our approval-seeking tendencies. Let's face it: We're all sinners in those pews. But if we're not willing to show our messy sides, why should anyone else?

On paper, the once-and-done walk of faith looks good, but it's unrealistic. I suspect that is why churches are filled with approval-obsessed people-pleasers—not only in the pews but in the pulpits. We don't want to admit we struggle, so we keep holding up the facade. Because we can't get over ourselves, and because we can't make any peace with ourselves, we try instead to *hide* ourselves.

"Dear God," I pray again, "help me get over myself—and get straight into Your presence. God, *get* me again, and again, and again."

Outside, the tractor rumbles through the field. And here, Christ cultivates one woman's heart—turning me right-side out for an upside-down Kingdom. I continue preaching sermons to myself, all through the day:

Pack school lunches. Remind self of God's truth. Repeat.

Fold denim and terry cloth. Remind self of God's truth. Repeat.

Flip through glossy magazine. Remind self of God's truth. Repeat.

See face in mirror, lined with middle age. See wiry grays peeking. Step on scale. Remind self of God's truth. Repeat.

At the grocery checkout stands, the soccer fields, the parent-teacher conferences, the class reunions, the job interviews—in all places and at all times, I keep at it: Remind self of God's truth. Repeat.

This is intentional, and it is not in our *nature* to do this deep, turning work. We need the Spirit's help to return daily to a place of repentance and renewal. One of my go-to authors on God's unrelenting grace, Brennan Manning, calls it a "steady self-confrontation."[2] In essence, as sinners, we must confront the idols that keep knocking on our front doors. Idols need steady confrontation. We have to hang a sign on the doors of our hearts, declaring to false saviors, "No vacancy."

Gospel preached, daily.

No-vacancy sign hung, daily.

Yes, we really *can* do this. Scratch that. Not you and I, but Christ who lives within us.

We are not who we were, and we are not yet who we are supposed to be. But we are surely this: We are becoming.

The tractor creeps up the hill, through fertile soil, preparing acres for seeds. A farmer's work is God's way of reminding us that great miracles can grow from something impossibly small. The Lord plants in the cultivated ground of human hearts these tiny seeds of grace.

I hear my daughter Lydia walk up behind me at the kitchen window.

"Morning, Mom," her voice croaks. She wraps her arms around me, leans against my hip. I pull her close, running my hand down her back.

I recall that day at the spelling bee, and my daughter's answer to a risky question: What would happen if she failed? "We would just go home," she had said.

An astonishing thing happens when mere mortals remember that crowns of incalculable worth await us in our one true Home. Suddenly, the world's applause resounds only as a clanging cymbal, when compared to the applause of the One who hardwired us for love.

I comb my fingers through Lydia's hair, untangling her silky, brunette locks. We stare out the window as the rising sun clothes our world in light. That green tractor climbs higher over the hill, leaving turned earth in its path.

And just when I'm getting okay with not being liked, I find out that I'm wildly loved.

It happens days later. I walk down to the mailbox under the canopy of ash trees on a warm spring afternoon.

Every day at three, Stan the mailman stuffs the mailbox at the end of our country lane. I open the flap, and the mailbox yawns with the usual fare: a Lillian Vernon catalog, a farm magazine, a handful of bills, and two invitations to sign up for credit cards. I tuck the mail under my arm, then walk up the driveway and into the house.

I am about to drop the credit card offers into the trash bin when a word on the outside of an envelope catches my eye: *preapproved*.

I look at it more closely, pushing my glasses up the bridge of my nose.

"You've Been Preapproved." The words are stamped in red.

I draw in a breath, clapping my hand over my open mouth. I blink twice.

That's the answer, right here in the junk mail—the answer to every insecurity I've had, every craving for love and approval, every race for significance. This is the antithesis to the Love Idol.

It's all there in that one word: *preapproved*.

I have been preapproved. Already approved. Already accepted. I have nothing to prove.

Seeing that word here in my hands, this truth that was mine to hold all along, I feel a familiar lump rising in my throat. I shake my head at the ridiculous and shocking gift of a Savior who loves us in spite of us.

What would it mean to know that I am *pre*approved? What does such truth hold for my life? It could seriously change everything.

I leave the garbage lid open, a hungry mouth. The garbage can is like the Accuser, who tries to swallow whole the truth about our approved status. How many times have I, in essence, thrown the truth in the garbage, letting the enemy gobble up grace?

The Bible. It's there on the table, so I flip it open. Ancient writ grips my soul in a new way. I turn page after page, on a scriptural excavation. I feel like I've struck gold, rereading hundreds of words that tell me that I have been, in a sense, preapproved. Only I never looked at it that way before. But now? I find one gold nugget after another—each of them satisfying a mortal's intense craving for love. It was right here all along, this series of "alreadys." How had I missed it? My eyes play connect-the-dots through all these promises—each one reminding me of what God has *already* done. And they are on practically every page. Past-tense promises for present-day believers:

I have already been forgiven (Acts 13:38).

I am already a co-heir with Christ (Romans 8:17).

I have already been chosen (John 15:16). And oh, how I wish I had known that when I was the last one picked for recess kickball at age ten, when I got dumped by a boyfriend at age twenty, when I didn't get the promotion at age twenty-five. God picked me!

And there's more. The pages rustle with confirming evidence:

I'm already significant.

"Even before he made the world," God chose me. And He loved me. Past tense. Before He created Mount Everest, the Great Barrier Reef, and Niagara Falls—before He even sent the globe spinning on its axis—He decided to love me, in Christ (Ephesians 1:4).

God already determined my role in this life, having prepared it "in advance," relieving me of the burden of having to plan my life out, as I've been prone to do (Ephesians 2:9-10, NIV).

I am already called His beloved child (1 John 3:1).

I keep going. Page after page, I see it: He is the God of Alreadys, inviting me to turn away from the voices that tell me I'm not "enough." His words are an invitation to every unwanted child, every unrequited lover, and every person who has ever wanted to know he or she matters.

Bent over these pages of Scripture, I remember the name of my worst critic: Jennifer Dukes Lee. Since childhood, I have told myself I'm less than. I have spent years in places like newsrooms and church sanctuaries, stretching to grasp the shiny fringe of some invisible standard. Even when it looked like I was wildly successful, meeting every demand of the Love Idol, that tyrannical false savior kept a new standard elusively out of reach, telling me:

You're not pretty enough.
You're not skinny enough.
You're not smart enough.
You're not funny enough.
You're not spiritual enough.
You're not house-cleany enough.
You're not [fill-in-your-own-blank] enough.

But God answers with a series of alreadys:

He tells me I'm already beautiful (Psalm 45:11).
I'm already "spiritual" (Ephesians 1:3).
I've already been picked (1 Thessalonians 1:4).

And He never once said I needed to vacuum before the houseguests showed up.

All day long, I can't stop thinking about it. I close the Bible, but I go about the day with the word on my lips: "preapproved."

I wash breakfast dishes and remember: I was already loved, even when I was dead in my transgressions (Ephesians 2:4-5, NIV).

I sweep up crumbs from the planks on the kitchen floor and whisper truth over myself and my children and every person who ever doubted it: He died for me—already—while I was still a sinner (Romans 5:8).

Long ago, the Lord said it: "I have loved you, my people, with an everlasting love" (Jeremiah 31:3). Past tense!

When I didn't know Him, He already knew me (Psalm 139:1).

God has been waiting with a fattened calf and arms wide open, even when I was "still a long way off" (Luke 15:20).

All of this. It could positively change a person's life.

I don't have to earn anyone's love or attention; I can turn around and receive Cross-bought love, freely given. Like the lost son, I can wear the ring on my finger and "the finest robe" (Luke 15:22), without worrying anymore whether it makes me look fat.

It's the essence of the faith into which I was baptized, the oath I uttered in confirmation, the prayers I've prayed since childhood, the creeds I've memorized and repeated, the verses I've learned by heart, and the songs I've sung since the days in the church basement when I wore my Strawberry Shortcake dress and patent-leather shoes.

I had been taught that Christ's love was something I already possessed, not based on my merit or good behavior or pretty prayers. I possess Christ because He took on Himself every sin I would ever commit. And He did that before I was even born. I was preapproved, in a sense, before my birth. He stamped me with a seal that said, "This one is Mine."

He died for me—a misfit who doubted His very existence—in the greatest act of validation known to

humanity. Before I believed in Him, He had already
died for me!

The gospel is more than nice words on a page, more
than mouthed abstractions about a Savior on Calvary. The
fact that I am already loved is the promise of an actual
Person, not a detached theological concept.

And to think that I had treated the Good News like junk
mail, like a glossy flyer or a cheap advertisement. I had been
reading the Good News—the best news story ever!—since I
was a child. I had heard it, read it, affirmed it, confirmed it,
tasted it, and sung about it.

But had I ever really believed it?

I'm not certain that I had.

But that loving Father of ours? He doesn't stop loving
us, even if we treat His message like garbage. Even if we
run away from home, demanding our inheritance and then
squandering it all (Luke 15:13).

I get the sense that God already had the party planned
before I turned back toward home. And He comes at me—
running straight for me. I can feel my heart thumping just
now, thinking of it. How a Love that was already mine
comes running. And He's been loving me all along.

I begin to see this too. God has been habitually leaving love
notes all over this privileged planet. For the whole lot of us,
for His Beloved. I begin to pray that I can see them, in the
everyday moments. I begin to read those love notes instead

of the ones from false saviors. I start listening to that one Voice instead of the inner critic. And I begin to set my affections more firmly on Jesus.

I am learning the love language I was made for.

This is not an "experience" or a "feeling." It is a living encounter with a living God. It is the certainty that God not only loves me, but He likes me.

He has planted His messages, like holy sticky notes, everywhere: in the rustle of the ash; in the steady burn of the sun on my back; in the spring breeze tangling my hair; in the song on the radio that brings me to tears; in the first wispy dandelion of the season; in the twinkling diamonds of a spring night, dumped out from a heavenly jewelry box. And they're all over the Good Book, of course. I read the shortest verse in the New Testament—"Jesus wept"—and tears fall while I sit in awe on my living-room couch.

All this God-love that has always been right here now compels me to notice.

I write the "alreadys" down in my journals, type them out on my computer, print them, and Scotch-tape them to my pantry door. I remind my children of God's love when they are left out at recess or slumber parties. I tell them again and again, "You are so loved." These become phrases we repeat to each other: "You've been preapproved." "You're already loved."

I can't stop telling anyone who will listen. I write about it on my blog, cataloging His love and goodness through story after story. I see God's love for His people in the most unexpected places—like nursing homes and rest stops and seat 12A on a Delta flight.

I pen these words from the seat of the plane, love letters back to the King:

We had our seat belts securely fastened and our tray tables in their upright and locked positions when we left. It was before dawn's first light.

We winged our way east—all four of us. I opened the shade of my window to predawn darkness and a thick fog.

I was thumbing through a Delta Sky *magazine, and Anna was resting her head on my shoulder. Then it happened: Heaven opened.*

In a glorious and simple moment that only a few of us noticed (because shades were mostly closed), we brushed up against the holy. The pilot had nosed the plane heavenward, through a cloud-blanket that covered the world in a dark, gloomy shadow. But here we were now, climbing into the light— suspended between two layers of clouds. And I swear, I could reach out and grab the hand of an angel up here.

All because we opened a window shade.

These are the times when we visit heaven before we really get there—a sort of sacred "trailer" for the movie that's been showing in theaters for, like, ever. It's proof that what we believe is real—and it's a sign that where we're going is already planted within us.

Yes, it's true, I tell you: Heaven is in us, even before we are in heaven.

We're learning heaven's language here on earth, if we're wise enough (or lucky enough) to be paying attention at the right time. Which, really, is almost any time. Heaven speaks to us, whispering the love language of our more permanent home into every corner of our temporary one.

And I am learning, and relearning, to open my eyes to this wonder—to open the shade even when it looks dark outside.

This is the spiritual reality undergirding my belief: I am unabashedly, irrevocably loved. And God is boldly broadcasting His love everywhere. I am opening shades in airplanes . . . and He is opening shades on my eyes. I am loved! Now. As is. And the more I focus on that love, the less I desire another's.

I am smitten.

When we read God's love notes, instead of the ones we've read for most of our lives in school classrooms and corporate boardrooms, we are "dispossessing the heart of an old affection."

Those are the words of the old preacher Thomas Chalmers. He said the heart needs something new to cling to, if an idol is to be properly evicted. "The only way to dispossess [the heart] of an old affection, is by the expulsive power of a new one."[3]

When we uproot idols, we make room for God. We discover a love that is *already* ours.

I stumble onto Timothy Keller's words: "If we are deeply moved by the sight of his love for us, it detaches our hearts from other would-be saviors. We stop trying to redeem ourselves through our pursuits and relationships, because we are *already* redeemed."[4]

God knows that we humans tend to forget, so He puts reminders in our paths—like strings tied around mortal fingers. It is why we are continually drawn back to the table of grace, where we remember with bread and wine that Christ died for us, while we were still sinners. The Savior *already* did that. Our job: to remember.

All this remembering, and recalling, and reminding . . . it really does feel like falling in love.

It happens at the Communion table, yes, but also out by the thistles and the milkweed, on the country road that heads toward home from the grocery store. One morning, I wake early to write these words on my blog:

> *This grand globe is but a covering for a very near and grander heaven. As surely as the Good Lord lives on high, He's knocking on doors inside people's bodies down here.*
>
> *I'm out on the gravel, with my two hands on the steering wheel, when it happens. I open that*

heart-door again. Sure, it was the song on the radio that started things. But mostly, it was God.

I've been feeling it everywhere: in the pew, on the beach, in aisle seven at Target. Or right now, kicking up gravel on the way back from the grocery store, with a gallon of milk on the passenger seat.

God knows no bounds, and worship can happen anywhere. Sometimes, Jesus comes knocking when you are wholly unaware of what you're about to encounter. I try to keep the heart-door ajar, because I don't want to miss any miracles.

God seems to favor the element of surprise, falling like dew on the skin, landing softly like a bird on a wire. And you look around to see if anyone else felt what you felt: an earthquake of the soul.

It happened like that the other day, on that quiet road, out past the Ter Wee farm and down by the Browns' pasture, near the tail-twitching horses and a single bird perched on a fence.

A song was playing, by Phillips, Craig & Dean. That trio ushered worship straight into my car—and into my heart.

It felt like the rending of an inner veil, from the top down. I—mere mortal, lowly sinner—dwelt in the presence of the King. Me . . . with my laundry detergent, my loaf of bread, my box of Pop-Tarts, and a grocery list stuffed in my back pocket.

I pulled the car to the side of the road and felt

that one tear fall down my cheek, while I yielded to a
Savior—out there, by the thistles, covered with thorn
upon thorn upon thorn.

It dawns on me, how I've wanted praise for myself. I've been a thief, robbing praise from the only One who deserves it. It's not my performance that matters; it is the Savior's. It's not what I can do for approval; it's what He's already done.

I don't want to make much of myself. I want to make much of Jesus.

∽෧෴

Weeks later, I read more life-giving words—this time from Pastor Tullian Tchividjian, grandson of Billy Graham.

I devour his words written in *Jesus + Nothing = Everything.* I underline the parts I like best—nearly half the book.

I had read about Pastor Tchividjian's own awakening to the God of Alreadys after he was blasted by criticism several years ago following his church's merger with a much larger congregation. By the time his family's summer vacation rolled around, he was absolutely spent.

"I'd always felt loved in church. Now, for the first time, I found myself in the uncomfortable position of being deeply disliked and distrusted, and by more than a few people. Now I realized just how much I'd been relying on something *other* than—something *more* than—the approval and acceptance and love that were already mine in Jesus," Tchividjian wrote.[5]

On his first morning away on vacation, he cried out to God in desperation, finding comfort and direction in the first chapters of Colossians:

> That June morning was when *Jesus plus nothing equals everything*—the gospel—became for me more than a theological passion, more than a cognitive catch-phrase. It became my functional lifeline. Rediscovering the gospel enabled me to see that:
>
>   because Jesus was strong for me, I was free to be weak;
>   because Jesus won for me, I was free to lose;
>   because Jesus was someone, I was free to be no one;
>   because Jesus was extraordinary, I was free to be ordinary;
>   because Jesus succeeded for me, I was free to fail.[6]

I underline his words and reread them, nodding. They reinforce all of the alreadys I've been uncovering. My mouth drops open when Pastor Tchividjian recalls the way that God spoke to him: "'Tullian,' he was telling me, 'you're *already qualified!* You don't have to make the grade on your own or seek more approval from anyone. In Christ, you're in!'"[7]

I cry when I read those words: "In Christ, you're in!" I am sad for all the ways that life could have been different if I'd been reading the right love notes in a sixth-grade classroom, a high school gymnasium, a college dormitory, a metropolitan newsroom. I was already loved, and I didn't even know it. Not really.

But here on a farm in Iowa, where ground is being cultivated in a new season of planting, I know that it is not too late to tend to fallow ground. It is not too late to worship the God of Alreadys, for my sake and for the sake of my children.

One night, just before bed, I am putting away dishes from the dishwasher. My husband is leaning back in the leather recliner with the remote in his hand, watching *American Pickers* on the History Channel. Our two daughters are playing Barbies in front of the fireplace.

I don't know it yet, but my older daughter picks up her dad's cell phone from the coffee table and texts me.

In the kitchen, my iPhone beeps. I set pottery on the shelf, then pick up my phone to read another love note. This time, my own daughter is God's stenographer:

"The Lord loves you, Mom. That was random, but it is very, very true. You are so loved."

God, who is right on time, is whispering it everywhere: "Jennifer, you've been preapproved."

How could reading God's love notes—whether in His Word or in this world—help you evict your Love Idol and make room for Christ?

CHAPTER 9

VERY LITTLE

Turn around and believe that the good news that we are loved
is better than we ever dared hope, and that to believe in that
good news, to live out of it and toward it, to be in love with
that good news, is of all glad things in this world the
gladdest thing of all. Amen, and come Lord Jesus.

FREDERICK BUECHNER

I AM STRUCK BY how freedom feels when it begins to wrap itself around the soul, like it fits because it was already mine.

I am struck by it on a Thursday morning, when I wake up with a wild mane of bed-head hair. My aching feet shuffle on the carpet, reminding me of my age in every step, and then I catch a glimpse of myself in the mirror. Sure enough, a dead ringer for Bob Dylan is staring back: me. A handprint is creased onto the left side of my face, and it won't wear off for another hour. My shirt is inside out, and I stumble over a basket full of dirty laundry.

Yet I feel completely and irrevocably cherished. The Love Idol is losing its grip on me, and this glorious freedom could change every relationship in my life—starting with the ones in my very own house.

It's 7 a.m. I head downstairs to gently shake my girls awake for school. Lydia feigns fear when she rolls over, like I'm the monster who lives under her bed.

"Nice hair, Mom," she says, with a deadpan voice and slow, blinking eyes. "I dare you to go to the store that way. Come on. . . . Remember what your book is about?" An impish grin stretches across her face.

I laugh, then ruffle her hair.

"Very funny, Lydia. . . . I will, but only if you go to school wearing a polka-dot shirt and ugly plaid pants."

She had arranged her school clothes on the floor the night before. Her smartly matched outfit—with belt and barrette—is smoothed out flat on the carpet, positioned in the shape of a person with one elbow crooked.

She is who she is—organized, tidy, high-achieving, and genetically predisposed to an approval addiction under the subclass known as perfectionism.

But we are both learning that a fine line separates perfectionism and excellence. We're trying to keep on the healthy side of that line, with God's daily nudging.

Lydia and I are learning that life in grace is about a Savior, not gold stars on a chart. Real life means we'll have ripped jeans, zits, messy hair, red marks on important tests, and flawed performances. So be it.

Lydia has been privy to the behind-the-curtain reality, not just the good act I sometimes reserve for the studio audience. She's smart enough to know when I've been read-ing bad scripts. But life is not a one-act play, and I don't have the energy anymore for rehearsed performances.

I have accepted the lead role in my very own reality show. It's called life, and it's all improv. No scripts allowed.

Without the crutch of phony performances, believers can make safe places for others to live life unscripted too: "We interrupt this program to bring you real life." Before you know it—*spotlight, schmot-light*—no one gives a hoot about who's strutting down the red carpet.

Lydia is persistent enough to hold me accountable to this new way of performance-free living. She'd make a bru-tally honest accountability partner, I tell you—one who makes sure that the words her mother writes in a book are the words her mother lives in real life.

She knows that I have committed myself to a life more satisfying than the one I had led as an approval-starved people-pleaser. She wants to hold me to my best intentions. And I want to do the same for her and her little sister. I yearn for us all to know the deep, deep love of Jesus—that it would be enough, that it always has been enough, and that it's a love that can never be overmatched by anything or anyone in this world. No one can outlove Jesus.

So we all go around this house, reminding each other that there are worse things in life than Bs on report cards and bad hair days. We remind one another that life in Christ is not a popularity contest—but a journey that confronts us daily with questions about the gods we will worship. We remind one another that God saw us before we were born, and He has "precious" thoughts of us, thoughts that "outnumber the grains of sand" (Psalm 139:16-18).

His love is not linked to our puny performances but to a Savior's performance on our behalf. It's elemental to the faith we confess every Sunday in our little country church: This life is not about us but about a God of unending grace and mercy. God doesn't stop at loving us. He *is* the Embodiment of love (1 John 4:8). Love is God's character toward us.

On this particular morning, I sit on the edge of Lydia's bed, smoothing out her polka-dotted comforter with my hand. Despite the evidence that would sometimes indicate otherwise (the person-shaped outfit lying on the floor, for instance), I do sense that she's changing too. She can still be who she is—attentive to detail, for example—without demanding the praise of her peers or teachers.

She has a math test today. She thinks she might get a B. I dare her to get one. She rolls her eyes.

I worry about her. If she gets less than an A, will her spirits collapse?

In parent-teacher conferences, her teachers have gently told Scott and me that if Lydia needs to work on anything, it is this: to let go of her desire to be perfect. So her father and I have talked to her, using those soothing, low-decibel voices and soft eyes that parents press into service when they want their kids to believe them. One night recently, Lydia said she wanted to get all those As because she thought we would be disappointed if she didn't. When she blurted out those words, I felt my heart twist inside my chest.

She does know that she is unconditionally loved *and* approved of by God and by her parents. Doesn't she?

We have told our girls, repeatedly, that *trying* your best and *being* The Best are two very different things. We don't expect perfection; we expect only for them to give their full effort. They don't need to earn our love; they already have it.

But subtly? Subtly, have we left a different impression? Scott and I both have type-A, approval-seeking personalities. Have we cut ourselves some slack? What behavior are we modeling daily?

In some knowing glance, or some mild body language, do we make Lydia and Anna feel disapproved if they come home with wrong answers on a worksheet or don't pick up their stray socks?

The night Lydia confessed her need for our approval, Scott and I tucked her in together, reassuring her of our love and approval, no matter what. Then we walked upstairs to the living room, sinking into the couch with sighs. We redoubled our efforts to make sure our girls both know they are valued simply because they exist, not because they perform to standards.

God worked through Lydia's science teacher. The teacher pulled her aside one afternoon, after she bungled part of a science experiment. She got an A-minus, and when he saw her crestfallen reaction to the grade, he followed her out of the room after class. Out by a row of blue metal lockers, he pressed a book into her hands.

"Read this," he said.

The pages were filled with good advice and a lot of exclamation marks. It was called *Be a Perfect Person in Just Three Days*.

The point of the book: The only way to be perfect is to do nothing at all. And what kind of life would that be?

"You're not perfect!" the author wrote. "It's ridiculous to want to be perfect anyway. But then, everybody's ridiculous sometimes, except perfect people. You know what perfect is? Perfect is not eating or drinking or talking or moving a muscle or making even the teensiest mistake. Perfect is never doing anything wrong—which means never doing anything at all. Perfect is boring! So you're not perfect! Wonderful! Have fun!"[1]

Right now, in Lydia's bedroom where the clothes are arranged precisely on the floor, I thank God for that teacher, Mr. Bruggeman. He is my daughter's very own Mrs. Huseman. I whisper a prayer that she will heed her teacher's wise words better than I listened to my teacher with her well-intentioned warning many years before.

And I determine that Lydia's eye roll won't be the final word this morning. "Would you be okay with getting a B on today's math test?" I ask, rubbing her shoulder as shafts of morning light slip through the window blinds.

"I'm *starting* to be okay with that, Mom." She sighs and

runs her hands along the hem of her pillowcase. "But it's hard, you know?"

Yeah. I know.

She reaches her arms up to me, throwing both of them around my neck, like she might actually mean it, but like she wants to know that I'll love her even if she fails. I hold her tight—tighter than I ever have. I can hug her all I want, but no matter what her teacher says, or her mother says, she must know it for herself, deep inside of her little body: She will always be a somebody in Jesus Christ.

The sun falls in long slats onto her bed, and I breathe in this moment—this embrace between two of God's kids, who are daily getting better. And always needing their Father.

❧

The girls are getting dressed, so I head upstairs to brush my hair. I look in the mirror at the real deal, as I try to tame that ungovernable hairdo. I brush; it resists.

I wonder right then whether a whole lot of people are pretenders, just trying to smooth out the wild and unmanageable parts of their lives. I mean, it might be a little thing: calculating a Facebook status to show one's best side. Or maybe it's something more insidious. I think of pastors who preach to the offering plate instead of to the pew sitters, who are desperate for more than nicely packaged words. I think of the approval-hungry wife, who wants to fit into one size smaller, hoping against hope that her husband will come

LOVE IDOL

back if she does. And I think of a sweet friend of mine, age thirty-three, who is still waiting for her father to whisper three words he's never said to her: "I love you." *And what if he never does?*

How many people aren't able to fully experience the love of God because they're waiting for proof from a spouse or a friend that they are worthy of love? How many people are living joyless lives of paranoia because they're afraid that the public will see how messed up they really are?

My mind snaps back to the night of an ice-cream social at the country church up the road. Scott and I weren't members there yet, but the event was open to the public. I remember how I stood in front of this same mirror, thinking I could cleverly hide my flaws. Anna had been born six weeks earlier. And this exhausted mom tried to cover up all of her postpartum blah with concealer and mascara. I slipped a striped dress, two sizes too big, over my head. I hoped it would hide the extra weight that I carried on my body and on my very soul. I was lonely, longing for a real friend—not someone who would give me the approval I craved but someone who would accept me as I was.

At the church, our family found open seats at the end of one of those long tables in the fellowship hall. And a woman named Michelle sat down beside me. She asked to hold the baby. Michelle and I had known each other casually, exchanging friendly waves on the highway between our homes.

That night at her church, Michelle saw someone whom

no one else saw. She saw underneath the fiction I had tried to manufacture at the bathroom mirror.

I thought I had been convincing. "Umm, no," she told me later with a chuckle. Not even a little bit. "God kept whispering to me, asking me to reach out to you, but I kept saying no. I wasn't brave enough. I'd never done anything like that. But He kept saying, 'Go.'"

Michelle remembered how a woman named Elaine had reached out to her many years earlier, back when she was a pregnant teen in a small town where people talked. Michelle hadn't forgotten what it meant to be shown Jesus' love at a time when she felt particularly flawed and vulnerable.

So she reached out to me. The day after the ice-cream social, Michelle and her husband, Rob, invited us over for dinner.

Soon, we became best friends; later, we joined that little country church.

Real had become our new black.

Perhaps the greatest gift Michelle gave me that first night was the reminder of who I am in Christ: not overlooked because I no longer had an impressive job title, not judged because I couldn't yet fit back into my old jeans, not expected to have it all together. When the apostle Paul told the Ephesians how to use their God-given gifts, he noted that "as each part does its own special work, it helps the other parts grow, so that the whole body is healthy and growing and full of love" (Ephesians 4:16). Michelle's faithful response to the nudge of the

Holy Spirit helped me heal and grow. I was reminded that, despite my insecurities, I was fully approved by God Himself.

I am well aware that many women never receive the gift of friendship that God gave me through Michelle. Many others go through their whole lives without being told by their parents that they are loved. The truth is, we may never receive the praise or love we long for from people. So while I am grateful for the friendship Michelle offered me, ultimately I couldn't look for acceptance from her. Nor could I seek it from my husband or my parents or my children. Their love is a beautiful reminder of the approval God has for me, but everything I long for is already mine *in Christ*.

That's why we need to be careful about expecting other people to meet our need for approval. The desire for others' love can become a substitute savior. Amy Carmichael's words echo in my heart: "If the praise of man elates me and his blame depresses me; if I cannot rest under misunderstanding without defending myself; if I love to be loved more than to love . . . then I know nothing of Calvary love."[2]

What love will we know and crave today? To whom will our hearts bow? Our answers to those questions— every single day—will help us decide whether we will chase after the Love Idol or the Love Author. They will also determine whether we'll wear the Real Us on the outside or tuck the most honest versions of ourselves away somewhere "safe."

I'm not saying that it's wrong to enjoy an accolade or to encourage someone with a compliment. There's nothing wrong with looking pretty or taking care of our bodies. It's not out of line to want our parents to love us. Nor is it wrong to hope that friends will include us. Those desires for love and acceptance may be perfectly healthy, but we have to continually ask ourselves, does our love for those things eclipse our love for Christ?

Henri Nouwen said it like this:

As long as I keep running about asking: "Do you love me? Do you really love me?" I give all power to the voices of the world and put myself in bondage because the world is filled with "ifs." The world says: "Yes, I love you *if* you are good-looking, intelligent, and wealthy. I love you *if* you have a good education, a good job, and good connections. I love you *if* you produce much, sell much, and buy much." There are endless "ifs" hidden in the world's love. These "ifs" enslave me, since it is impossible to respond adequately to all of them. The world's love is and always will be conditional. As long as I keep looking for my true self in the world of conditional love, I will remain "hooked" to the world—trying, failing, and trying again. It is a world that fosters addictions because what it offers cannot satisfy the deepest craving of my heart.[3]

If my cravings take a controlling position in my heart, an idol is growing. My life has proved the theory true.

Here at the bathroom mirror, I turn on the faucet, wetting down this unruly mop of hair. I do wonder if a lot of us are part-time posers who want to break free but are too scared. And maybe we're all just waiting for someone in our own circle to drop the facade, to get really real. Then everyone else would have permission to do the same. C. S. Lewis once said that friendship is born in that moment when one person says to another, "What? You too? I thought I was the only one."[4] I know there's truth in Lewis's words because I've observed it in cramped Sunday school rooms, where women hunch nervously over Bible study workbooks. One woman risks her vulnerability, admits her weakness, and pretty soon, the whole room is nodding in agreement. Someone passes a box of tissues, and everyone grabs one in a communal act of tearful release. We draw strength from the honesty and vulnerability that come from friends and fellow believers. Together, we can help each other smash the Love Idol.

But who will be the first one to unzip her heart and grab a tissue right here today?

I will.

And it's not because I'm some great hero. Jesus is the only hero in any room where I've ever stood. But I have often tried to take away the praise that was His all along. It's a nasty habit.

I turn off the bathroom faucet, set down the hairbrush,

and then walk to the kitchen because Bob Dylan needs to make two little girls breakfast.

I pop frozen waffles in the toaster for the girls. This new life is for my sake, but also for theirs. We are all mirrors. What—or rather Whom—will I reflect?

The girls finish their breakfast. I wipe syrup from two chins and twenty fingers. We tie shoes, grab light jackets, and fail to find the missing library book. Together, we walk down our country lane, under that canopy of ash trees, to wait for bus no. 44.

Lydia, Anna, and I stand in a circle, holding hands. "I'll start, Mommy," Anna says. She begins our morning prayers as a gray-striped farm cat named Pretty Kitty weaves through our legs. "Dear God, thank You for the food and drinks, and help us to have a spectacular day."

This has been our morning ritual for several years. Before the bus stops at the end of our dusty lane, we pray. We've begged God's mercy for sick cats, missing mittens, poor people in Haitian villages, mean girls at recess, tsunami victims in Japan, cranky substitute teachers, and better school lunches. Today we also pray for Lydia's math test and for her willingness to accept something less than a perfect performance.

We end our prayer in Jesus' name, thanking Him for loving us "no matter what."

The bus pulls up, and the girls climb into its mouth.

They're swallowed up by the rolling, yellow beast. I watch them waving at me through dusty windows. The driver hauls my babies to school—a sort of training ground for a Western culture that values straight As, flawless skin, expensive cars, and athletic prowess. These are the things that compete for God's love.

I turn and walk back up the driveway, gravel crunching under my tennis shoes. I've been a sucker for what the world has to offer. I've been Exhibit A for John Calvin's assertion that human hearts are well-oiled idol factories.[5]

Timothy Keller says you can spot an idol by recognizing how it makes you feel on the inside. "An idol is whatever you look at and say, in your heart of hearts, 'if I have that, then I'll feel my life has meaning, then I'll know I have value, then I'll feel significant and secure.'"[6]

I'm in the middle of a great substitution, expelling the Love Idol and replacing it with Calvary love. I walk through the back door and head straight into the office to study.

On my computer, I click on the Bible software icon, then type in "1 Corinthians." It's in that book somewhere, I think—a reminder of how Paul regards the opinions of others. I'd heard it in a sermon online once by James MacDonald, in which he called our kind of problem a "bottomless ditch" and a "consuming bondage."

"When you live to please people," MacDonald said, "even the most important people in your life like your mom or dad or boss or spouse, you will be caught up in a bondage that can consume your life."[7]

I scan through glowing pixels on a computer screen. And there I find the verses that were the basis for his sermon:

> As for me, it matters *very little* how I might be evaluated by you or by any human authority. I don't even trust my own judgment on this point. (1 Corinthians 4:3, emphasis mine)

Paul, the former approval seeker, wrote that the opinion of others was not only a little thing but a *very little* thing.

A "very little" thing for Paul needs to become a very little thing for you and me, every day.

I say the words out loud, because I need to make them personal. "It matters very little how I might be evaluated."

If we are criticized today, what does it mean? Very little.

If someone challenges our parenting today, what does it mean? Very little.

If someone corrects us, disagrees with us, or talks poorly of us to others, what does it mean? Very little.

And this: If someone endorses us, applauds our work, affirms our parenting, or offers us praise, what does it mean? Very little.

When you and I no longer rely on praise or approval for our performance, we find new freedom: We can enjoy affirmation without craving it. Because it has lost its grip on us.

I flip through Tullian Tchividjian's book again. I had highlighted these words: "We no longer need to rely . . . on the position, the prosperity, the promotions, the preeminence, the power, the praise, the passing pleasures, or the popularity that we've so desperately pursued for so long."[8]

I grab my journal to write myself a short note—something that has become daily practice. Today's entry:

Dear Jennifer,

It matters very little how you might be evaluated today. (1 Corinthians 4:3)

Love, Me

Months ago, Monica, a friend in Colorado, had mailed me this handmade journal bound loosely with string. I looped three words on the front in black ink—"Letters to Myself"—on the day I first started writing in it. I figured I could write one short note to myself every day—a brief pep talk to help me discern the difference between the big things and the "very little" things.

On the first page, Monica had written these words: "You are in Him, He is in you." That was a very *big* thing.

On that first day of writing letters, I grabbed a pen and scrawled these words on the page:

Dear Jennifer,

Do us both a favor today: Don't sweat it. Cut yourself some slack. And be gentle to us. Resist the urge to compare. And club those niggling insecurities over the head. When you get to thinking you're not enough, keep in mind that Christ died for us, "while we were yet sinners" (Romans 5:8, KJV). We've been preapproved!

Love, Me

And so began these continued, daily evictions of the Love Idol. I sense that my approval-o-meter, while not yet smashed to smithereens, might be shrinking. And when one "very little" thing is made smaller, it makes room for Someone much greater (John 3:30).

~~~

Sometimes it's two steps forward, one step back. But it really does feel like a long series of steps in the right direction, doesn't it?

Even on the days we're not "feeling it," we must stand firm. One morning I write:

Dear Jennifer,

God created you and declared you "very good"—not perfect. . . . 'Nuf said.

Love, Me

I do feel less like a slave to the little things that have hounded me for years. I have been willing to try new things, at the risk of failing. I've dared myself—and my daughters—to get Bs. I have been more willing to laugh at myself and to make mistakes publicly. I've felt less of a need to explain myself or to defend my actions.

Dear Jennifer,

No offense, but today I'm going to focus on Jesus so much that I kind of forget about you.

Love, Me

When a trusted friend calls, I openly share my insecurities, rather than asking all the questions as a way to deflect attention from my own flaws. Last Christmas, for the first time in years, I didn't feel obligated to send out cards as some act of self-preservation or social requirement. I also didn't feel the need to deck the whole house with boughs of holly; instead I was able to focus on the Person whose birth we were celebrating, not the decorations.

And most important, my mind has become less preoccupied with the opinions of others and more interested in the exultation of God. I'm replacing my craving for self-esteem with a deep longing for Christ-esteem.

In John Piper's words, the Love Idol shatters when we begin to "make much of God" instead of wanting others to make much of us.

Is not the most effective way of bridling my delight in being made much of, to focus on making much of

God? Self-denial and crucifixion of the flesh are essential, but O how easy it is to be made much of even for my self-denial! How shall this insidious motive of pleasure in being made much of be broken except through bending all my faculties to delight in the pleasure of making much of God![9]

When we make much of God, we no longer yearn for someone to make much of us. Opinions matter "very little." We no longer desire praise for our performance. If someone has something nice to say, well, that's all it is: something nice. We can enjoy affirmation without craving it. Because other people's opinions have lost their power over us.

And on the flip side, we can take the criticism that someone might dish out at us—or that we direct at ourselves—without letting it ruin our day.

Dear Jennifer,

When you try to tell yourself how "ungreat" you are today, replace every negative thought with how great our God is!

Love, Me

Yes, tiny miracles happen when we die daily. Every small death of an idol is another tiny resurrection of our identity in Christ. And every small death only happens in the shadow of a bigger one. That's the thing about the cross of Christ.

When we go to Golgotha (literally, a "heap of skulls"), we are spiritually rebooted.

Returning daily to the cross of Christ, to a place of death, is the way to life. It is the only place people can pin their sin, including the self-destructive sin of approval seeking.

We slay the Love Idol at the site of the Crucifixion, nailing it to the cross.

This is why the communion of saints gathers at the altar. Every other Sunday morning, we serve Communion in our white-steepled country church. I shuffle toward the bread and the cup, along with Michelle and Rob, Art and Rosie, Helmer and Hazel, Trish and Bill—all of us sinners, all of us silently confessing our messes, but doing so shoulder-to-shoulder, in community. We are publicly standing with Christ, and with one another, when we put small thimbles of wine to our lips. And when we whisper these words to one another—"This is the blood of Christ, shed for you"—we are the body of Christ, taking a sledgehammer to the Love Idol.

Dear Jennifer,

May the gospel of Christ get bigger in you today.
Love, Me

At 4 p.m., the bus creaks to a stop at the end of the driveway. I meet the girls halfway under that bright blue dome of sky. Our world declares the love of a Creator.

Lydia sets her backpack on the gravel, kneels down to unzip it, and then pulls her graded math test from a glossy folder. She is smiling. It is a broad smile that covers the whole lower half of her face and stretches up to crinkle her eyes. She hands me the paper, folded in half, as we stand there under those rustling trees, where the sunlight filters through fresh-budding branches.

I unfold that one sheet of paper, my eyes darting to find the grade, and sure enough, there in the corner is the most beautiful letter in the whole wide world: B.

Why does making much of God make it possible for you to care "very little" what demands your Love Idol— or anyone else, for that matter—places on you?

CHAPTER 10

CUPPED HANDS

You don't think your way into a new kind of living.
You live your way into a new kind of thinking.

HENRI J. M. NOUWEN

I REST MY CHIN on our farm gate and puff out a breath of frustration. Two Angus calves with saucerlike eyes stare back at Lydia and me. On this June morning, we are chin-deep in a showdown at dawn.

These cows simply won't budge, refusing to drink from their buckets. The water's skin flutters when a lone fly drops in for a landing.

Lydia and I cajole the calves with mothering voices. Lydia chirps a rhyming tune:

Sherbet and Daisy,
Don't be la-zyyyy!
Come drink from your pail of waaaa-ter!

But those two unyielding black calves with wet noses simply blink long eyelashes at us. I scuff at the dirt with the toe of my boot.

What they say about horses is also true for cows: You can lead them to water, but you can't make them drink.

Lydia wears worry in a knot above her brow. Her shoulders tense up with an unspoken question: *Will these calves ever learn to drink from a bucket?* Lydia kneels down, swirling the water into figure eights with her index finger. I lean beside her, rubbing reassurance into her back with tiny circles.

"It's okay, hon. We'll try again tomorrow, all right?"

Our chore pail, hidden from the calves behind the hay bales, holds two supersized bottles—the kind you'd buy if you were raising a baby Goliath or a newborn Bigfoot. Until the calves learn to drink water and eat starter feed from buckets, they will nurse from these bottles. We had hoped they wouldn't be needed today, but the calves are winning this battle of wills.

Lydia's resignation tumbles out of her mouth with a heaving sigh. She relents and marches for the hidden bottles. With her jaw clenched, she grabs a bottle of milk replacer to feed Sherbet; I take one for Daisy. We hold the bottles through an opening in the farm gate, bracing ourselves as the calves lunge at us, full tilt. These baby brutes are ravenous, like Augustus Gloop lurching toward Willy Wonka's chocolate river.

The county fair is eight weeks away. By then, the calves

must be weaned. One of these graceless, 120-pound beasts will, theoretically, learn to walk behind her 55-pound surrogate mother, Miss Lydia Lee. Using a rope halter—a kind of leash for bovines—Lydia will lead Sherbet or Daisy around the 4-H show ring on a late July afternoon.

Or so we hope.

It all looks a little daunting at this point. Through the farm gate, these calves tug at their bottles with slobbering mouths. Within minutes, they drain the bottles dry and beg for more with pleading, blinking eyes.

I look down at Lydia and reassure her, "They'll learn. They'll wean eventually."

I speak with the calm confidence of someone who knows what she's doing. But it's a slippery confidence and—*snap*—just like that, it's gone.

An old familiar ache rises up as I hear a sneering reproach in my head.

It goes like this: *Woman, admit it: Here's yet another farm chore that's beyond you.*

It's just a small thought—inconsequential, really. But it's right here, in these maddeningly mundane moments, that old insecurities like to make unannounced visits.

My husband—the real farmer on this farm—is helping me learn to be gentle with myself. He encourages me to try new things, like bottle-feeding calves with our daughters, even though I sometimes feel like a clumsy and inadequate farmwife.

He simply laughs and shakes his head when I retell the

story of how I got myself and Daisy tangled up with the rope halter. The rope is supposed to fit over the calf's head. But I somehow slipped it on backward, and it wound itself around the calf's neck. Meanwhile, the other end of the rope circled both of my knees and one of Daisy's legs. We eventually got ourselves untangled, and while I can safely say that no animals were harmed in the making of this paragraph, my pride might have been a bit bruised. Yet Scott's good-natured response to my foible reminds me how God looks at us—"in process" and lovable, despite our mistakes.

Without regularly reminding myself of God's unquenchable love, I might be inclined to let my lousy insecurities tangle themselves like rope halters around my heart every time I make a mistake. My daughters might do the same.

Old idols are stubborn, showing up in innocent places like calf pens—exactly as they did in my grade school classrooms, corporate cubicles, and department-store dressing rooms during swimsuit season.

I do realize that at times the Love Idol still slithers up beside me to hiss its lies into my ears, especially when I'm lacking confidence in my performance. This recognition is a victory in its own right. But still, I wish the Love Idol were permanently silenced.

I've come to learn that, even after it's been muted, the Love Idol is just looking for an opportunity to ambush each one of us. Here's how it finds its opening:

People can hear a thousand times that they are deeply loved by the Father, the Son, and the Holy Ghost, but each person's attention so easily transfers to another trinity: Me, Myself, and I.

Even the disciples suffered from misaligned vision. They jockeyed for position. They craved approval and significance. (And these were the guys who rubbed elbows with one-third of the Trinity on a daily basis.)

On Jesus' last night on earth, those friends gathered around a table with Him. Christ broke bread, calling it His body. He lifted the cup, saying it was His blood poured out.

Christ predicted His betrayal and death. The clock was ticking toward the most important event in human history. But the disciples didn't concern themselves with the calamitous events ahead for their Friend. Instead, "a dispute also arose among them as to which of them was considered to be greatest" (Luke 22:24, NIV).

How long did it take for their attention to transfer back to themselves? Before the plates were cleared? Before they choked down one more bite of bread? It's horrific to consider.

In the twenty-first century, we find ourselves mimicking that same self-focused behavior. Yet here's where amazing grace proves itself amazing once again. God never gives up on us, even when we act like self-centered buffoons.

God is astonishingly patient, daily correcting our near-sightedness. He woos us to take our eyes off ourselves and put them onto Christ, every day. He means for us to turn fully to Christ for our approval, the One on whom "the Father has placed his seal of approval" (John 6:27, NIV).

Furthermore, God's Word compels us to choose the Holy Trinity, not the self-centric trio of Me, Myself, and I. We are to fix our eyes on Jesus (see Hebrews 12:2).

I have sung that old Helen Lemmel hymn for years:

Turn your eyes upon Jesus.
Look full in His wonderful face.
And the things of earth will grow strangely dim
In the light of His glory and grace.[1]

Look *full* in His wonderful face, the song commands. I ought not merely *peek* at His wonderful face, or glance, or scan. *Look full.* And behold.

When we look full into the face of our Savior, our myopic focus shifts from our own selfish interests. The things on earth really do "grow strangely dim."

And so at the calf pen, I take a deep breath and let it out slowly, remembering—*this is not about me.*

We will need to remember that when our personal trinity joins in with the enemy in an ugly song of insecurity and fear. It's an amplified chant, trying to drown out the love song of the Father. We have to actively turn the dial to tune in to the frequency of the Father's love song. And then we can hear it, the One who sings over us with love (see Zephaniah 3:17).

True—God's love song has already awoken me from my childish stupor and my trancelike attentiveness to human approval. And yes, I have gladly fallen in love, again and again, with a Hero who sings of His love, all the way to that one scandalous cross placed high on a hill. He loved me then—two millennia ago! This overwhelming already-love has astounded me, has drawn me to tears. I've heard the exquisite song of salvation, sung over sinners straight down through the ages, straight into forever, and straight into me. But I have to continually adjust the inner dial to hear the melody, because my old nature wants to sing the foul refrain of self-doubt and insecurity.

I stare at these blinking calves. I would consider giving away two five-gallon buckets, a pair of manure-caked boots, and one stubborn calf to the first person who could provide me with bulletproof answers about how to permanently muzzle the Love Idol.

Then again, I doubt that even Jesus Himself would suggest bullet-pointed answers to life's most pressing questions. He didn't outline easy steps for us; He offered an easy *yoke*:

Come to me, all you who are weary and burdened,
and I will give you rest. Take my yoke upon you
and learn from me, for I am gentle and humble
in heart, and you will find rest for your souls.
For my yoke is easy and my burden is light.
(Matthew 11:28-30, NIV)

Farmers of an earlier generation understood those verses about yokes in literal ways. Old-fashioned yokes consisted of a bar with two loops—either of rope or wood—that connected a pair of animals who worked in tandem to pull a plow.

We don't use yokes on our farm. But I'm recalling that day when I clumsily got tangled up with Daisy. When I wear the yoke of the world, I can get myself all twisted up with a beast. That's because the world's yoke is not easy or light. It is heavy, weighed down by pride, self-promotion, success, and our desperate hope that someone will approve of us.

The yoke of craved-for love and approval is like dead-weight. Charles Spurgeon knew it. That truth thundered down from his pulpit in 1886:

You want to get on, to be rich, to be famous and all of that! But is that Christ's yoke? He says, "I am meek and lowly in heart." Ambition is your own yoke, not His! And the lust of wealth, the desire for power, *the craving for human love*—all that is a yoke of your own making—and if you will wear it, it will gall you. There is more joy in being unknown than in being known and there is less care in having no wealth than in having much of it. We often go the wrong way to work in seeking true restfulness and happiness.[2]

Over one hundred years later, I nod my emphatic yes to Charles Spurgeon. I put on Christ's yoke by setting my heart on Christ again, instead of on myself. In that same sermon, Spurgeon tells us how to identify the yoke:

> The yoke of Christ is His word, His precepts, His commands, the following of His example, the bearing of suffering which He appoints, the persecution which comes to us for His sake.[3]

The morning sun spreads out a carpet of light through the gaping door of the calf shed. Lydia grabs two armfuls of hay, and I open the creaking gate for her.

God is holding me close, even now, when my soul eyes are trying to refocus on Him. One booted foot rests against the rail, and I am looking up.

Christ never asked us to follow a series of easy steps; He asked us to follow Him up the hard road to Calvary. He never once asked us to pull ourselves up by our own bootstraps; He asked us to stay in step with Him, so close that He can feel our breath on His back. I want to get that close.

And if we stray? God comes back for us. He never lets go when we're in process. Never. God has never put anything between us and His love, except for His Son.

God is not suddenly going to abandon what He started in us at birth. Paul wrote, "I am certain that God, who began the good work within you, will continue his work until it is finally finished on the day when Christ Jesus returns" (Philippians 1:6).

Those words from Paul do not give us permission to deliberately repeat mistakes. But the apostle's words do remind us that we suffer from the chronic condition of what's commonly known as being *human*. And we need to be gentle with our weak selves.

I know it as sure as I'm standing here at the gate with two stubborn calves. We're the same way—proud and rebellious. Our peace can drain fast, like milk from a bottle. We need a holy refilling. We daily need God's grace and Christ's gospel to blunt all the bullheadedness of our humanity. The goal of the journey is not to be perfect in this life but to *meet* Perfect. When insecurities make unannounced visits and start to heckle us, we have to deliberately turn our backs on them.

As I walk to the other side of the calf pen with chin held high, the morning sun warms me through.

I breathe deep and look full. I look full in His wonderful face. With the Spirit at work in me, I choose:

Christ-esteem. Not self-esteem.

Christ-awareness. Not self-awareness.

Easy yokes. Not easy bullet-pointed steps.

More helpings of grace. Not a buffet of self-condemnation.

A chorus of God praise. Not cries of despair.

God's glory. Not my own.

I don't want to live all pharisaical, loving "the glory that comes from man more than the glory that comes from God" (John 12:43, ESV).

I whisper it to the heavens, words lobbed straight up, as Moses did: "Show me *Your* glory. *Your* glory, Father" (see Exodus 33:18).

And what is God's glory? What did Moses see when God's glory passed by?

God didn't show off by puffing out His chest with power or might or brute strength. His glory didn't appear like the selfish glory of the American dream. It was the loving character of God passing before Moses. The Lord didn't even show His face; He showed his *back*! The Lord showed His glory through His goodness and love and mercy:

> The LORD said, "I will cause *all my goodness* to pass in front of you." (Exodus 33:19, NIV, emphasis mine)

When we ask earnestly to see God's glory, He responds with reminders of His infinite compassion and mercy, not a power play. He speaks of all the ways He is good and all the ways we are treasured. He reveals Himself with these vivid reminders that we are *already* loved.

On this morning, God's glory comes, quite literally, out of left field—this farm field planted in evenly spaced rows of corn, acre upon acre.

There is no magic formula for this, no rubbing of a genie lamp or snapping of the fingers to make it so. But when her eyes look full on Christ, one weak woman is overcome by a holy moment, a marvelous brush with a sacred presence. I know how crazy this sounds to the skeptics. I've been one of them. But it really happens. Right here, in the most ordinary place—which smells of sweet hay and manure—I come face-to-face with glory. Glory wings its way onto my skin, coming on the morning summer breeze, hovering over my soul, then tickling invisible strings on the inside. His goodness passes by, and I am aware of an irresistible Savior, loving me.

This is holy God, whispering, "Consider Me. Look how much I love you."

When we're feeling unapproved and insecure, our culture has an answer for all of us: the Wow Factor. We are told to wow people with our looks, our wit, our Facebook statuses, our bank accounts, our children's accomplishments . . . even our snarkiness and sass.

But what the world offers—apart from God—simply doesn't satisfy.

What if we became less interested in wowing others and more focused on being wowed by God?

God is right there, waving His arms, saying, "Look! Look! See what I've made for you here? Look around you, every day, at the ruddy cheeks of your very own children, and the dazzling night sky, like diamonds on velvet, and the ruby ripple in the Communion cup."

I think of the example of Christ, who never sought His own glory. He split open the cosmos and fluttered to earth in a dirty place reeking of manure and livestock—a place not unlike where I'm standing now. His mother wrapped her baby snugly and then laid Him in a manger. The Son of God *in a feed trough*! I shudder to think of it. His birth would not merit a mention in the newspaper's society pages. Who applauded His birth? A group of ragtag shepherds.

At first glance, the Savior's arrival looks like a marketing disaster. But this was no mistake.

Jesus' entire life was marked by humility, not status. People continually urged Him to produce the miracle, the Wow for the crowd. Yet Jesus repeatedly asked those around Him not to tell anyone about His miracles. He warned them not to worship the Wow Factor but to worship the God of Wow.

He was a King with a dream—not for Himself but for His Kingdom. No one uncorked the champagne in the garden of Gethsemane. Not a soul rolled out a red carpet. Jesus Christ *became* the red carpet, laid low and bent over with agony, sweating drops of blood.

That's the way God's "Wow" often looks—wholly sacrificial.

Under a wide-open sky unfolding itself to heaven, I offer a silent prayer of gratitude.

And Satan flees in the presence of praise and adoration and the glory of God.

The Creator hoists that yellow orb higher in the sky, turning green fields into gold and burning away the silky morning mist. I am a prospector, wanting to scoop up all the gold and carry it in my heart. My own cheeks flush, and I close my eyes, letting a love song sink in. I can hear the world awaken, with crickets and cows and rustling aspen leaves all making a hypnotic morning rhythm of glory. Of love.

My daughter is humming a made-up song while she gently slides the halter over Daisy's head inside our little red barn. And it's like a holy finger reaching down to touch the mesmerized heart of this woman in muddy boots, who has conveniently forgotten about herself in exchange for a view of glory, out here by a manure-reeking barn.

God's glory supernaturally recasts even the most rancorous parts of this world. But I only have eyes to see it when I forget about myself.

Timothy Keller calls it "the freedom of self-forgetfulness." Or to paraphrase Keller's definition of humility, we don't think less of ourselves, but we think of ourselves less. "True gospel-humility means I stop connecting every experience, every conversation, with myself. In fact, I stop thinking about myself. . . . A truly gospel-humble person is not a self-hating person or a self-loving person, but a gospel-humble person."[4]

I need to forget myself right here, right now, when I doubt my worth as a farmwife.

I have to forget myself when I get snubbed by friends, or when I feel flabby and wrinkled, or when I get a critical note in my in-box, or when I am trying too hard to make a good impression. I must forget myself when Satan whispers, "What will others think of you?"

I've had to forget myself in far more painful situations: when friends betray, when hoped-for love does not come, when I'm shunned, when someone shames instead of uplifts.

Those moments can defeat us or define us. We might look at the evidence, these shards of a broken life, and allow them to convict us as unworthy of love. We might let human rejection convince us that Satan is right: We really are unloved and unapproved. We could let our mistakes shame us into dark, quiet corners. But no, Jesus won't have it.

When the Love Idol jeers, when we feel like losers, God answers back, "You are *not*."

Christ continually shouts through the universe, "You have a love that is already yours. You have nothing to prove to anyone. You have nothing to prove to Me. You are significant and preapproved and utterly cherished. Not because you are 'good,' but because you are Mine."

Take that, Satan.

Keller asks, "How can we worry about being snubbed now? How can we worry about being ignored now? How can we care that much about what we look like in the mirror?"[5]

This is what God does, this God of all glory and dominion who reaches down with a holy hand to lift our chins and turn our eyes toward the Son, so we may look full in His wonderful face and "forget ourselves."

Beyond the gate, this scroll of fields unrolls in God's glory.

All of it pours forth like a song, like a chorus from this Father who won't stop loving us: "I love you. I love you. I already love you. And I'll sing it to you again tomorrow, because I never want you to forget it. You are My beloved."

And I believe it.

∽◎∾

Two calves' tails twitch. Wide, begging eyes plead, *More*.

Both bottles have been sucked dry. Defeated, Lydia and I walk up the hill to wash before breakfast. Just as these calves will one day be weaned, God is weaning me.

In the mudroom, I turn on the faucet and wash bottles. Milky water swirls down the drain.

It feels like a sort of inner cleansing, an act of faith, to stand here at the sink, watching dirty water drain away. It's an inner turning, a refocusing, a flipping over.

I have to remind myself daily what I already know: Focus on the Father, not on my flaws. Look to the Savior, not the self. The Messiah, not the mirror. This is the power of the gospel: Water cleanses, through the Word (see Ephesians 5:26).

I feel victorious in Jesus, having made the conscious choice to drink from Living Water instead of the bottled praise of humankind. "Yes, like a weaned child is my soul within me" (Psalm 131:2).

A patient Father can lead His child to water, but He doesn't make her drink it. He holds water out, as if in cupped hands. He bids her, *Come and drink*.

And at the edge of this sink, where all the grime has drained away, I drink again from those hands. I sing back to the Father, and I look full in the Savior's wonderful face, soaking in the beauty. I repeat memorized Scripture about who I am, about how I've been fashioned by God, created to do good works that will bring His Kingdom glory, here below. There is no earthly yardstick, rating system, ticker, or scale to measure *that* sort of worth.

The water runs clean, and I can feel it now—how when I've shifted my focus, anxiety drains away. This is what I have been learning and relearning: Look upward, not inward.

It's real. And it's really changing everything.

The Lord didn't ask for us to prove our significance to the world. Or to prove ourselves to Him. He didn't ask us to prove anything at all. *He* is the One who approves, declaring us beloved. Christ asks again for our whole hearts and our willingness to drink Living Water from His cupped hands.

Just then, it dawns on me. *My hands.* I turn off the faucet and call for Lydia. "Come quick, honey! I've got an idea. I think I know how to wean Sherbet and Daisy."

She pulls on her boots again, and I tell her what we'll try. She's giddy with hope, giggling a stream of joy all the way back down the hill. The gravel crunches under our boots. A barn swallow swoops overhead. The morning breeze whistles in our ears.

The gate creaks open with an easy push, and we call out for the calves. "Sherbet, Daisy!" They peek out the barn door with those blinking saucer eyes.

"Will it work, Mom?" Lydia asks. "Will it work this time?"

I bend down on my knees beside a five-gallon bucket. Two calves step closer, curious and tentative.

I dip both my hands into the tepid water. If they won't

come to the water, then I can bring the water to them. I lift my cupped hands, filled with water, like a chalice. I inch forward on my knees, with those hands held out as an invitation, and then I slip water under the wet nose of one still-thirsty calf.

And right then—from cupped hands stretched out on an early morning, in this common place where God's glory slides like gold across the water's surface—it happens. A baby learns to drink.

How might your Love Idol try to make a comeback if you focus on the unholy trinity of "Me, Myself, and I"? In what ways does God offer hope if you find yourself bowing down to that idol once again?

CHAPTER 11

BLEACHERS

We are the women who make our lives about the cause of
Christ, not the applause of men, live to express the Gospel, not
to impress the Jones', live not to make our absence felt, but
to make Christ's presence known. We are the women
who know it's not about us and all about Glory.

ANN VOSKAMP, "THE SONG FOR ALL THE WOMEN"

"HOW MANY PEOPLE will be in the bleachers?"

I hear the faint outline of fear hanging in Lydia's voice when she lobs her question into the manure-scented air of the 4-H barn. The place is filled with the lowing of cattle and the lazy buzzing of flies. Lydia bites her lower lip. And Anna puts a hand on her sister's shoulder, a soft reassurance.

The bleachers in the show ring are, indeed, packed. It's a standing-room-only crowd. Denim-wearing farmers with sunburned arms have propped their boots up on the gates around the show ring. These farmers will press in for a closer inspection when the livestock strut around the ring.

Soon the announcer will call out across the loudspeaker for Lydia's age category to appear in the center. Here in the calf barn, Scott kneels in the hay so he can look Lydia straight in the eye. He wags a finger and says, "Don't you worry about who's in the bleachers, all right? You just have fun out there."

Twice today, Lydia will go eyeball-to-eyeball with her inner critic, the one who tells her she might fall or fail— or both.

The first arena: the 4-H show ring with Sherbet the calf.

The second arena: the spelling-bee stage of the Lyon County Fair, that place where she previously unshackled herself from her fear of failure. She came away with a ten-dollar prize and a heart full of confidence.

It dawns on me just now. The spelling bee was exactly one year ago today. And this is the very barn where I had chosen words similar to the ones her father is sharing now. Lydia and I had walked under this very roof, hand in hand, past bellowing calves and hay bales and blue ribbons on our way to the spelling-bee stage. I remember how I asked her if she'd be okay if she lost. An hour later, she walked off that stage as the champion.

Lydia is a spelling-bee whiz but a show-ring rookie. Her dad squeezes her hand. "Just enjoy this, Lydia!" These are the same words he spoke to me, when—with shaky confidence—I began to write this book.

Lydia is learning what her mother has also discovered: The idols from which she's being set free often threaten to ambush her soul again. She and I may well keep fighting some of these battles until we take our last ragged breaths.

And here in the barn is Anna, shyly standing in her sister's shadow. Anna has been a silent witness to this wrestling match between Lydia and the perfectionist's curse. In some ways, I wonder how much Anna has quietly influenced her sister and me with her carefree acceptance of who she is. At a young age, she is not afraid of mirrors or report cards or bleachers. I do worry that the world will try to wring the innocence out of Anna, but for now, she seems somewhat resistant. This is a gift, and I thank God for it.

Anna pats her sister's shoulder.

Our family of four circles in tighter, sitting on scratchy hay-bale seats while we wait for Lydia's turn in the ring. The air is thick, like you could cut it with blunt-tip scissors. Even the flies seem too hot to fly. I brush a lethargic bug from the top of Lydia's head.

Time has folded over on itself, it seems. A span of years has become a series of mirrors, and I see a reflection of myself that looks a lot like Lydia. On a daily basis my daughter must fight against her own people-pleasing tendencies. As I tucked her in one night, she told me, "It's in our *bloooood!* Mwa-ha-ha-haaa!" Our chests rose with laughter, jiggling the bedcovers, and she held up her hands like they were beastly claws. We laughed until tears streamed down our faces.

Honest to goodness, we have learned to laugh at ourselves. We've even learned to poke fun at our perfectionism. And when we don't, little Anna does. "Lydia would *not* approve of my locker," Anna will say to us, pointing to the wooden space in our laundry room where she keeps her coat, boots, a stack of random papers, a dirty sand bucket filled with pens, a few coins, a pair of broken swim goggles, and several of the household's missing socks.

Laughter has been good medicine. So are the daily reminders of how dearly God loves us as we are, not as we think we should be.

The girls and I still go around reminding one another that we are already loved and approved—regardless of ribbons or grades or accolades or the present condition of one's locker. Who knows? Maybe we will always have to remind each other. There could be worse things, I guess, than reminding a person how dearly she's loved by the King.

Lydia has come so very far. She's wrestled those itchy insecurities all over our little corner of the world: down by the calf barn, straight up onto the spelling-bee stage, right through the angst-ridden homework sessions, and all the way to the occasional B grades on tests. She's fought hard against approval and peer pressure in places like school buses and playgrounds. Earlier this year, when the youngest children on her bus were afraid to stand up to someone saying mean things, Lydia risked her approval rating, marched straight past her fears, and reported the behavior to the school principal.

She had made the decision without any coaching from her parents. We had no idea, until her teacher sent us an e-mail that morning: "It takes a very strong person to come forward. She could have just sat by and let it continue, but she did something about it!!!!"

Every word and every exclamation point bore the mark of our daughter's emerging bravery.

Here in the cattle barn, perspiration runs in rivulets down our backs. I scoot closer to Lydia on the hay bale to remind her how far she's come. How far we've *both* come. And how we were just crazy enough to try something like raising a calf for the fun of it, regardless of whether we won or lost! I retell the story of how I tangled myself and Daisy up in the ropes and was mortified that our neighbors might see the barnyard spectacle. A wider smile sweeps across her face, then disappears.

"But what about the knot, Mom? What if I mess up the knot?"

Only a few minutes earlier, we'd found out that 4-H exhibitors were expected to tie their calves to a gate using a special farmer's knot. It's a complicated series of twists and loops in the rope, but Lydia picked it up quickly and confidently—then she practiced twenty more times to be sure. (Because, you know, she's my kid. God bless her.)

But the time has nearly come for her to enter the ring. The announcer will be calling her age category soon. Lydia is as prepared as she can be. She has mastered the knot, has brushed her calf again and again, has picked away bits of hay from Sherbet's legs. And I watch how she keeps smoothing down her own hair again and again—a nervous habit she inherited from her mother.

We have been so busy preparing and preening, we almost forget to pray.

So, together in the barn, our family of four bows heads before God, asking Him to calm that jumpy, spirited calf in the ring full of noisy people. We pray for peace over performance. Anna prays that her sister will get a pretty ribbon. And her dad? He prays that she will just have some fun.

After we say our "Amens," I keep praying silently for Christ's strength in her weakness. That is a prayer that God seems heaven-bent on answering.

Down through the annals of human history, God has demonstrated a proclivity toward bursting onto the scene in people's weakest moments. He's consistently the caped hero—like a real-life Superman—who makes a name for Himself through the feeble and frail. I know. It sounds a little crazy, but it's true: Christ shows favoritism toward human weakness. "My power works best in weakness." That's what Jesus told Paul, the recovering perfectionist and approval seeker who wrote most of the New Testament. Paul began to believe those words so deeply in his core that he began to *boast* in his personal weakness (see 2 Corinthians 12:9-10).

Paul knew what Lydia and I have begun to learn: Personal strength is not necessarily a virtue. Neither is got-it-togetherness. Clearly, Christ has a soft spot for weaklings. He repurposes human weaknesses, using them as doorways through which He escorts great power. Then there's no question who gets the applause before the final curtain falls.

"How many people will be in the bleachers?" This was the question Lydia had asked her father and me.

I understand the hyperventilating trepidation behind that question. What if we fall, and people actually see it happen? What if we mess up in front of a live audience? Sure, Christ promises to be our strength. But He never promised to make *us* look good. Our whole lives are built to glorify our God, not ourselves. Even Christ didn't want the glory for Himself (see John 8:54). He even commanded people to keep His jaw-dropping healings secret (see Mark 7:36).

Are we willing to open our lives fully, to be used for God's glory and not our own?

I remember the way my friend Patty once dared me to pray: "Dear God, let my words and my life honor You. I'm willing to fall flat on my face if it brings glory to You. In Jesus' name, amen." I began to pray that prayer before speaking engagements, because the podium was one place where I wanted to "perform" flawlessly.

Only later did I recall the saying "Be careful what you pray for."

Here's why:

One morning, before speaking to a small group, I repeated the Patty Prayer. A few minutes later, I was striding toward the podium. While walking up the steps, I tripped on the hem of my pants in front of the people gathered in the pews.

As I fell down, the room heaved with one collective gasp. But then I stood up and, though red-faced, managed to quip, "I have this habit of falling for Jesus again and again."

I still pray the Patty Prayer. Not because I hope to repeatedly embarrass myself, but because it's one prayer that has changed everything. It's my pledge to be obedient, even if it means I might look like a fool. It's my way of telling God—and reminding myself—that this life is about God's glory, not mine.

And now it's Lydia's turn to step forward, despite her weakness.

The sun filters in through the open-air barn on the county fairgrounds. The calves moo and moan, shuffling to find shade.

Lydia bends her head down toward Sherbet's ear, whispering like she might be able to sweet-talk her calf into behaving in the show ring.

"They're ready for you," her dad says.

Determined, Lydia unties her calf, and with her dad's help, she escorts Sherbet between the barns, weaving her four-legged brute toward the opening of the ring. Anna and I squeeze in between the capped farmers at the gate. I wring my hands.

The crowd clucks and coughs and murmurs, a low-pitched hum of excitement. A thick layer of sawdust covers the show ring. At dead center, the dour-faced judge spreads her feet out, standing in a wide stance with her hands on her hips. She motions with one hand and a slight nod to the exhibitors. The crowd hushes.

I strain to see my girl and find her through my camera lens: my firstborn with number 122 pinned to the back of her 4-H T-shirt. It startles me how she's grown up so much in this last year—even in this last hour. Her hair flows down her neck, and her chin is raised in a pose of determination. I see courage in those hands as she grips the blue rope that she'll use to lead Sherbet around the show ring.

She and Sherbet enter the ring. They complete the circle, finding a spot by the show-ring gate as the judge stops to examine each calf. The judge will ask each child, one by one, to tie his or her calf to the gate.

It's Lydia's turn now, and I can see how her hands are shaking, just a bit, while the judge looks over her shoulder. Lydia repeats a series of memorized loops and twists, then pulls the rope through one last time—just like she learned.

Yeee-ES! On the inside, I quietly cheer.

The judge tells her something, but I can't quite make out the words. A crestfallen look spreads across Lydia's flushed face. Her chin falls to her chest.

The judge moves on to the next calf exhibitor. Lydia scans the crowd and finds me at the gate. She mouths the words to me across the ring: "I did the knot wrong. I did the knot wrong."

I mouth words back. "It's okay. It's oooooo-kay."

"I did the knot wrong," she repeats. The corners of her mouth droop.

I pray, *Lord, just let her get through it. Be her strength.*

Suddenly Sherbet bucks and backs away from their spot at the gate. Lydia's eyes widen with surprise, and she grips the rope hard. She turns Sherbet around twice, trying to regain

control of this feisty calf. And then it happens—*whump*—
Lydia loses her balance and falls in the sawdust. She reels
back on her haunches and steadies herself with one hand,
right there in the show ring with a room full of spectators.

She falls.

I watch, stunned. I want to rescue my girl. I want to run
into the ring and pick her up, dust her off, and help her
out of the gate. But I don't. I stand still. Because it's not my
place to be her strength in this moment of weakness. I pray
under my breath, "Dear God, give her strength, give her
strength, give her strength."

And then, within seconds, Lydia stands. She doesn't let
go of Sherbet. She stands. She brushes herself off.

I can see how she's holding back embarrassed tears and
swallowing down the lump in her throat. Hardly anyone
noticed, I'm sure of it, but she's wearing a look of humilia-
tion, like the whole world saw this one fall. Like Satan might
just be whispering, *What will everyone think of you now?*

Then she moves back to her spot. She throws her shoulders back, lifts her chin up, and stands tall. I try not to
make eye contact with her so I won't break the confidence
she excavated from somewhere deep inside her small self.

On the other side of the ring, the judge has finished her
evaluations. She approaches the announcer's microphone.
Eighteen blue and red ribbons are stacked on the table,
along with one champion ribbon and one reserve champion ribbon for the second-place finisher.

The microphone crackles as the judge congratulates

everyone for a fine showing. Then she calls out the champion. He's a ten-year-old boy with a broad grin, and the crowd applauds as the winner steps forward to collect his purple ribbon.

I steal a glance at Lydia. She's fine. *She's actually fine!* She's up and standing, holding fiercely onto that calf. She didn't win. And she's fine anyway, praise Jesus.

The judge speaks again, to announce another champion in that circle of exhibitors. The announcer calls out the name of a girl who prepared and prayed and feared the worst. She calls the name of the girl who fell but stood back up again.

"Our reserve champion this afternoon . . . is Lydia Lee."

The local paper's photographer shoots a few pictures, and our family trades high fives and hugs. Then we tie up the calf at her place in the barn.

Another stage waits for Lydia Lee. The Lyon County Spelling Bee is about to begin.

Last year, I was full of advice. This year? I won't say a word. No suggestions. No reminders. I will be a quiet cheerleader, watching rather than directing.

At the registration, Lydia writes her name on the line. She encourages me to sign up for the adult spelling bee, raising her eyebrows, tilting her head, and using her favorite accountability phrase with me: "Remember what your book is about, Mom."

I cross my arms over my chest and, laughing, tell her that the attempt at a book is sort of like my very own spelling bee. Who knows, I might even misspell *misspelled* in the manuscript.

Lydia capitulates, and I'm off the hook for another year's spelling bee. (But if you're holding these words in your hands, apparently I'm not off the hook for the book.)

We take our seats on a long wooden bench near the front of the room. Lydia asks for a quick review of the spelling-bee rules. Her father tells the story of his fifth-grade spelling bee. Scott Lee—son of a farmer—was eliminated on the four-letter word *bale*, those round bundles of hay that dot the Iowa countryside. He spelled it *bail*.

Lydia giggles. I don't sense the nervous agitation that burdened her last year. Maybe it's because she won the year before. Is she overconfident, determined to win again? I'm not sure yet.

Two rows behind us, we hear a mother and daughter having the same kind of conversation Lydia and I had a year ago. The child is reluctant. Lydia knows the girl.

"Should I talk to her?" she asks in a whisper. But before I answer, Lydia stands up and walks two rows back.

I can hear Lydia behind me, trying to convince the girl that it's not scary at all, really. And that it's actually kind of fun. And who knows? She might be surprised to find herself the winner, but first she'll need to try.

She returns to her seat and whispers to me, "I don't think she's going to do it. Maybe next year."

The announcer is onstage now, tap-tap-tapping the microphone to test it.

Quickly, Lydia asks me to pray for her while she's onstage. She laces her fingers into a ball under her chin and then whispers earnest words: "But Mom. Do *not* pray that I win, okay? Promise me, Mom, that you won't pray that I win. I mean, it's okay if I win. But don't pray for that. Just pray that I'm not too nervous."

It's time. The announcer has called twenty fourth graders to the stage.

"I'll pray, Lydia. I promise," I tell her, patting her leg. Then off she goes, this little girl who is living proof in a four-foot-two-inch package that, in Christ, people are mighty overcomers.

I feel a lump in my throat, a lump of sheer pride, watching my girl ascend those steps again. She sits up straight in the first row, confident. She waits for her turn at the microphone.

She nails the first word—*salmon*.

The second word, *February*, could be tricky, but she remembers both *r*'s and advances to the next round.

Round after round, more contestants walk off the stage, until only three children remain: Lydia, a boy, and another girl. It's the same girl who lost to Lydia one year ago, on the word *valleys*.

Right there, in the championship round of words, I whisper prayers to the Father—not that Lydia will win but that she and the other children onstage will appreciate the opportunity they have been given to experience the joys of life. And maybe I'm praying that prayer for myself too. It's more than a petition to the Father; it's me saying, "Thank You, God." This is a prayer of gratitude to the Lord, who has brought us this far, encouraging us to try new things and take pleasure in life, without the burden of having to perform or "get it right." The created world—a gift to mortals—is fertile ground for playful, daring hearts. And I've only really begun to let my inner adventurer enjoy it, so that I might live life more fully, more courageously.

As parents, Scott and I encourage our girls to do the same—to take piano lessons or to turn a cartwheel; to try rolling sushi or to enter a poetry contest. Even if they fail or fall.

And we're encouraging ourselves to do the same—raising calves, writing a book, running a half marathon (despite my lack of athletic prowess). We're not trying to do it right; we're just trying to *do* right. There's a difference.

Our adventures are also taking us outside of our comfort zones. Scott has stepped into ministry with prisoners, and both of us have taken separate trips to Haiti. The girls began asking this summer if they could go someday too.

It's not always a big thing, like a mission trip or a book. Often it's a very little thing, right in our own neighborhoods.

Take Christmas Eve, for example. My husband and I found ourselves standing side by side in our country church as part of a brass quintet. Never mind that neither my husband nor I had played brass in twenty years. True, I had to search for "French horn fingerings" on Google to refresh my memory. We could have said no. But we wanted to be part of a magical moment. (Well, I did anyhow. I had to talk Scott into playing that banged-up, borrowed trumpet.) But it was in that spirit of adventure that my husband and I picked up the instruments in a burst of musical bravado. Yes, we sounded a bit like sick elephants during our first rehearsals in the living room. But Christmas Eve came.

The pastor had instructed us to play our song two times through. With forty-two sets of eyes on us, we lifted borrowed horns to our lips, and the opening strains of "The First Noel" filled the sanctuary.

And no kidding, we sounded like a real band. I did hit at least one wrong note, and I lost my breath midway. And after only one verse, we all lowered our horns. Between bursts of laughter, we decided one verse was plenty.

It wasn't great. But, man, was it ever fun.

If you scroll back through your life, you might find that your fear of disapproval has blocked your playfulness. Maybe it's because you have felt the sting of rejection and self-doubt too many times.

If you're not careful, you could stop trying anything that seems scary or dangerous—little things, like playing the French horn, or momentous things, like being a parent. The perfectionist's mantra is this: If you can't do it right the first time, don't do it at all. Let your new mantra be this: Do it anyway, even if you fall. Pray the Patty Prayer, and then walk brave.

When you belong to Christ, honest to goodness, you are free to make mistakes.

That new mantra has brought Lydia and me back here, to the spelling-bee stage on a hot July afternoon.

I watch now, as my daughter listens while the announcer pronounces her next word: "Pleasant."

Lydia draws her mouth into a knot, tilts her head, and looks up toward the ceiling, like she might be able to pluck the letters from the rafters.

She nods. She thinks she's got it. Then, her answer rolls out with the confidence of a winner.

"Pleasant. P-L-E-A-S-E-N-T. Pleasant."

The woman shakes her head no. Lydia has misspelled the word. My daughter looks puzzled but walks off the stage, as instructed.

She comes toward me with her hands upturned, as if asking what went wrong. I cup my hands around my mouth and whisper in her ear. "It's P-L-E-A-S-A-N-T. You had an extra *e* in there. Great job, though, Lydia. I'm so proud of you!"

She sits between her dad and me, and we both squeeze her shoulders.

She lost.

Only she didn't.

This was a huge victory. She didn't pray to win. She just

prayed for a little strength to make it through. And she did. She made it through. This is what we prayed for.

The spelling bee continues two more rounds, until the last speller is left standing—the girl who lost to Lydia the previous year. This girl is about to be declared the winner of this year's Lyon County Spelling Bee.

But first, she'll need to spell one last word correctly. She stands up a little straighter, like she knows she'll get this one right. And she does. She spells it just right:

"Prayer," she says. "P-R-A-Y-E-R. Prayer."

The girl won on a prayer.

I watch Lydia sitting on her hands beside me. I wait to see what she'll do next. Because I've come to know this truth: A person being loosed from the Love Idol is no longer envious of others in the spotlight. She is free to genuinely appreciate the accomplishments of others; free to stop comparing and jockeying; free to celebrate others' victories, rather than wish them for herself.

And this might just be what freedom looks like: this brunette girl of mine, standing up tall beside me to applaud the new winner on the stage.

*How might acknowledging your weaknesses
and taking risks anyway diminish the hold
the Love Idol has over you?*

CHAPTER 12

HAITIAN HALLELUJAH

At the end of life, we will not be judged by how many diplomas we have received, how much money we have made, how many great things we have done. We will be judged by, "I was hungry and you gave me something to eat. I was naked and you clothed me. I was homeless and you took me in."

MOTHER TERESA

OUR DAUGHTERS' foreheads are pressed against the cool, oval windows on opposite sides of our southbound jet.

Scott and I exchange nervous glances across the aisle of the plane. (To clarify, *my* glance is the nervous one.)

"This is crazy," I whisper to him.

"Crazy enough that it could only be God. . . . No worries." A wide grin stretches across his face, and my "God's Got It" farmer reaches across the aisle to squeeze my hand.

We are taking our girls to Haiti.

Yes, *that* Haiti. Third-world-country Haiti. Poorest-nation-in-the-Western-Hemisphere Haiti.

In about an hour, the plane will begin its descent onto a

tiny island of tent cities and anemic villages, a proverbial stone's throw from our approval-saturated lifestyle.

Minutes ago, we left behind the Florida shoreline swollen with mansions and backyard swimming pools. Wouldn't it have been easier to take the kids to Disney World, "the Happiest Place on Earth"?

I know the answer to that question, despite the parental anxieties that I am mouthing across the airplane aisle. In the last year, Scott and I have traveled on separate short-term mission trips to Haiti. The country is paradoxically one of the most impoverished and most joy-filled places on earth.

The country and its people have captured our hearts. We support two Iowa-based mission groups in Haiti: a nonprofit organization called Touch of Hope and a job-creation ministry called Vi Bella Jewelry.[1] And we are praying about other long-term opportunities to join God in His work in Haiti.

Our family of four didn't come alone on this trip. I turn in my seat to look down the aisle for two familiar faces.

Five rows behind us, our best friends, Rob and Michelle, wave back at me. This isn't their first trip to Haiti either. Rob and Michelle traveled there a few months after the earth-quake in 2010.

Our trips to Haiti have extended from a growing aware-ness of God's love and grace in our own lives. Over the years, God has awakened soul places in each of us that we didn't know were asleep. Christ has been a lion in our hearts, snap-ping us out of hypnotic trances with a holy roar of love.

How could a comatose heart not be wildly altered under the power of such affection? Christ's love is positively world changing. We can't keep this love to ourselves. Christ's holy commission commands us to tell others. Spread our joy. Pour ourselves out. Love somebody, outrageously, in Jesus' name.

God didn't create His beloved to be stingy hoarders. He fashioned us as love carriers and couriers, sending us to the ends of the earth. Or maybe right across the street.

When believers come to know God's love heart-deep, we are compelled to live into that love *life*-deep. To be pre-approved means this: We love *from* our approval, not *for* our approval. We love without expecting anything in return.

"Go!" God tells us. "Your heart has been untangled from the false distortions of love. You are no longer tied down by fears of rejection or disapproval or popular opinion. If you forget how much I love you, which you probably will, do not lose heart. Turn back to Me, and I will remind you how much you are treasured. Then I will send you out again with a command: Love your neighbors as yourselves."

God has been uprooting the Love Idol from my life, freeing me from the bondage of people pleasing, perfectionism, and approval seeking. *Praise Jesus.*

But let me be frank: He didn't go to all that work merely so I could feel better about myself. There is far more at stake here than my fragile ego. Christ didn't convince me

of my preapproved status in this life just so I could feel
more at ease in my size-ten jeans next to the moms wearing
size-four skinny jeans. He didn't go to the trouble of vali-
dating my worth merely so I could feel better about myself
as a farmer's wife, a mother, a writer, or a church volunteer.
In the end, this has nothing to do with me at all.

This really is all about Jesus. And Jesus is calling us to
respond, in His name, so that when we show up in heaven,
we can stand before Him completely poured out and breathless, with flushed cheeks, all in the name of love.

Our family has been asking God to give us eyes to see the
people whom we can love more fiercely than we ever dared
before. And lo, they are everywhere. In church pews, prisons,
city parks, nursing homes, preschool classrooms, cemeteries,
the Target restroom, backyard barbecues, the corporate
boardroom, my own kitchen, my very own mirror.

And in Haiti.

A few weeks before we left on our trip with the girls,
I read the words of Oswald Chambers in my dog-eared
copy of *My Utmost for His Highest*: "Are you ready to be less
than a mere drop in the bucket—to be so totally insignificant that no one remembers you even if they think of those
you served? Are you willing to give and be poured out until
you are used up and exhausted—not seeking to be minis-
tered to, but to minister?"[2] My answer: *Dear God, I beg
You, make me willing.*

For years, the world has had a terribly powerful effect
on me. My love for lesser gods has eclipsed my love for

Jesus. And it's prime time for me to tip the scales: for me to have more effect on my world than it is having on me. But I want to do it in a way that doesn't eventually turn the focus back on myself. If I'm going to write stories or books, I want to write them for *God's* glory. I want to love my next-door neighbor for *God's* glory. I want to be a part of significant, life-changing work in Haiti for *God's* glory. I want to resist the worldly urge to take even a smidgen of glory for myself. That would be stealing.

Thousands of feet above the ground in this airplane, I stroke Anna's hair as she looks out over our great big world.

We are so eager for the girls to see what we've seen: how the poor have untold riches that you can't stuff in a billfold. Some folks compare Haiti to hell. Call us crazy, but Rob, Michelle, Scott, and I believe we've found a slice of heaven on that little island. We've found a new way of seeing our world because of the Haitian people. In important ways, they are the richest people I've ever met. But we aren't blind to the gut-wrenching poverty.

As we zip through the air, I think back to my first trip to this country. One day stands out: We had spent the morning walking from one house of sticks to another. We stopped to touch scabbed faces and to pray over babies with swollen bellies. We dropped to our knees along dirt paths to greet naked, hungry toddlers who still managed wide grins when we greeted them with glad *bonjous*. They threw their spindly arms around us. The path led us higher up the hillside, past skinny donkeys, past the hunched and the hacking, past the little boy with a shirt that read, "It seemed like a good idea at the time."

We huddled under tattered tarps flapping atop wizened sticks. We prayed for a five-year-old girl, her arms and legs askew like her whole body had been broken. Her mouth opened into a giant oval, and her eyes were rolled up like window shades, so we could see only the bloodshot whites. Her parents told us she'd been that way since she was one year old, but they weren't sure why. A fly landed on her cheek, and she couldn't have brushed it away, even if she'd wanted to. So I swept my fingers across her cheek, one slow glide, to shoo away the fly. Moments later, another fly landed between her eyes.

It all looked so hopeless, like the pointless work of shooing flies. Like God had forgotten this part of the world, maimed and marred by natural disaster, poverty, trafficking, and the atrocities of corruption. I remember thinking, *How does a human being read God's love notes here, in a place like Haiti? How would a Haitian ever know that he is approved and loved by a living Creator? Where is the proof?*

That same morning, we visited a family of five living in an eight-by-eight hut with loosely thatched walls. Their home clung to a scrubby hillside. The floor was wall-to-wall dirt, and the family officially had nothing—unless you counted the two crates pressed into service as chairs and the green bucket used to haul water.

The man of the house sat on one of the crates, like he was folded in half. His knees touched his chest, and a threadbare pink T-shirt hung like a loose drape over his gaunt shoulders.

I looked into his face, lined with the hardness of years lived in Haiti. My tongue was heavy in my mouth, and I felt thirsty—for water, yes, but mostly for answers. Did Haitians like this man wonder if God had left them alone, favoring the comparably wealthy short-term missionaries who occasionally walked through their villages with thousand-dollar cameras draped around their necks?

A question tumbled out of my mouth before I had a chance to think about what I was asking: "Sir, what brings you joy?" As someone translated the question, I gazed down at the Haitian man's mismatched shoes— though shoes might be too generous a term. They were the soles of shoes, tied onto his feet with ratty strings.

And I had the nerve to ask him about joy?

After the man responded to my question in his native Haitian Creole, the translator turned back to me and gave me his answer: "My joy and my strength come from the Lord Jesus Christ. My joy comes because I just took another breath."

His words hung like silken threads in the air—a hope that was resilient to poverty and pain. It's a hope you could see only with your heart—not your eyes. Human eyes wanted to focus on the single buzzing fly, the tattered tarp, the dirt floor. But in this little shack, God's love was magnified through one man's testimony of joy.

After we prayed together, it was time for me to go.

I squeezed the man's shoulder and said, "Bondye renmen ou." Translated: God loves you.

And he nodded his head. He already knew.

Does a human being with *nothing* have a better chance of learning that Jesus is *everything*? Is my life of excess actually one way to *starve*? I do wonder if my own privileged upbringing has been one of the biggest obstacles to finding true significance in this life. Unchecked, it could stand in the way of the next generation too.

Corrie ten Boom, a concentration camp survivor, knew that truth. She once wrote these words: "You can never learn that Christ is all you need, until Christ is all you have."

Corrie's words aren't hollow abstractions of a faith learned in a church basement. They are professions of a life lived and a love learned in the despairing trenches.

Before we left on this trip, Rob, Michelle, Scott, and I had traded numerous stories about Haitian people who are living testimonies to Corrie ten Boom's words. So many of our Haitian friends exude unspeakable joy, despite their worldly circumstances. We had been part of three-hour-long worship services in Haitian churches, where the poorest of the poor praised God as if He had appeared in the flesh at the pulpit. We had met numerous believers in tiny stick-framed shacks whose unadorned lives were evidence that real joy can be found in Christ alone—outside of earthly pleasure, praise, popularity, or power.

And now it was our daughters' turn to see. I prayed hard that they would.

❧

The plane begins its descent.

Lydia whips her head around. Her eyes, flashing and bright, tell me what her heart feels. She is smitten.

"It's just . . . beautiful, Mom. More beautiful than you told me it would be."

The tin and tented shantytowns blur beneath us. We fly over whole communities heaving with chaos and pain. But she first sees the beauty: a turquoise sea and this jagged crook of an island, which cradles more than ten million souls. We're close enough now to see the foam on the shore.

Beside me, Anna reaches for my hand and pulls it to her chest, holds it so close that I can feel her beating heart under her ribs.

If I could hear her heart right now, I wonder if it would sound like this: *Jesus . . . Jesus . . . Jesus.*

With a thud and a roaring rush, the airplane skims across a concrete ribbon in Port-au-Prince, then glides to a stop. A voice crackles from the cockpit microphone, welcoming us to Haiti. Someone on the flight crew unseals the door, and the warm air grabs us with an unidentifiable, untamed odor. My heart races in expectation.

We walk down a long hallway in the Toussaint Louverture International Airport, toward a jolly group of musicians who greet us with maracas, guitars, and banjos.

I wonder how our girls will make any sense of what they see when we step onto the city streets and the dirt paths.

It's sad enough to watch the pain of poverty on your TV screen, but soon the pain will stand within inches of the girls' noses. Within hours, that pain will have a face. Poverty will want to hold the girls' hands and will beg for a drink of water.

How will two American children, accustomed to bulging cupboards and endless cereal choices, even begin to process the jutting rib cage, the tin roof, the always-bare feet? What if the girls hate it here?

This is the moment when American parents might second-guess the decision to bring their two kids to a third-world country. But we know what we are introducing our girls to. We've seen the chaos sitting next to the beauty, the suffering propped up next to the sacred.

We pile our suitcases into the back of a truck driven by one of our friends from Touch of Hope. The engine belches, and we tear off down a long, cracked road that carries us out of the city. It's a road that promises to change us all.

Haiti becomes a blur of fruit stands, half-dressed toddlers, and slumped buildings that serve as unwitting monuments to the 2010 earthquake. We drive past a mass grave that entombs thousands of earthquake victims. The grave, widely photographed after the earthquake, is now covered in thick brush and marked by a cross near a place called Titanyen. In Haitian Creole, the village's name translates to something like "less than nothing."[3]

But it's not the macabre that the girls want me to see. They tug at my skirt and ask me to behold the beauty.

"Mom, look! Look!" the girls shout over the roar of the truck, as we drive through villages that overlook the bay.

I am pretty sure the girls are not in denial of the poverty around them. You can't help but see that here. But they can't stop smiling: at a woman balancing fifty pounds atop her head; at brightly painted buses called *tap-taps*; at a mother hanging her family's colorful wardrobe out to dry on cactus fences, like an arcing laundry rainbow; at backpacked girls in matching uniforms, with fat ribbons curled up in their hair.

"It's just so beautiful, Mom," Lydia says again and again.

All of us in the truck know that we will see the ugly soon enough. The ugly will make our hearts twist in our chests. You can't avoid that pain in Haiti. But right now, it's like the girls know they would have missed Haiti entirely if they didn't pay attention to the beauty.

I can sense it: a fresh kind of love growing up from deep inside of the girls. And inside of me.

We've been on Haitian soil less than an hour, and we pull off the paved highway to bump down a narrow road heading toward the ocean. In the distance, I can see the bright yellow school buildings of Touch of Hope in Simonette, a small coastal town about twenty miles north of the capital city. This is our first stop, and the girls' eyes widen.

Our friend parks the truck, and the girls leap out, racing toward slides, swings, and a merry-go-round.

This is the playground that love built.

Four months earlier, Lydia and Anna had dreamed of raising enough money to build a playground and basketball court for the Touch of Hope school. It would cost seven thousand dollars to build both. But they were determined. Their motto: "Every kid deserves to play."

Just as Scott began to harvest our fields, playground dreams took root in the cultivated soil of our girls' hearts. They began a fund-raising effort by selling Vi Bella Jewelry and homemade soy candles. We told all our friends on Facebook and Twitter. And those friends told their friends. The story got picked up by daily newspapers and TV stations in Sioux Falls, South Dakota, and Sioux City, Iowa. By Christmas, all the money had been raised. And then some.

Now, here we are. The girls are racing toward the playground. Their hair tangles with the air. They climb the jungle gym, zip down the slides, pump their little legs to make those swings go higher. They test-drive the merry-go-round.

I mostly stand watching, and I cry the happiest cry ever. Lydia fans her arms out, in one giant sweeping motion across the playground, and she spins toward me. "It's beautiful, Mom. Just beautiful."

Let me be frank. I am no hero. I am no Katie Davis or Christine Caine.[4] Neither am I a model mother with perfect children. My cupboards and dresser drawers are far fuller than I need them to be. Our well-fed family is comfortable and warm. Our girls fight over the iPad. When we get home, they will still push peas around on their dinner plates. And me? I still white-knuckle my white-picket-fence life more than I should. I have to daily wrestle down the Love Idol.

But God is opening our hearts to ways that we can love others, no strings attached, wherever He takes us, at home or abroad. When we're busy loving others, we don't have time to fuss over who is—or isn't—loving us.

When I bowed down to the Love Idol, I was only this: a noisy gong or a clanging cymbal. I think how the "love verses" in 1 Corinthians 13 might read if I could add my own contemporary lines today.

Maybe like this:

If I speak about God's love, but do not share His love with others, I am only a blabbering blogger.

If I want to be noticed and demand the praise of man over God, but have not love, I attain nothing.

If I look in the mirror, but see only my flaws, I've learned nothing.

If I write a book about approval, but continue to compare myself to others, I have gained nothing.

Love is patient and kind. It does not envy or compare or covet another's Coach purse. Love does not bury one's own God-planted dreams in the gutter of fear and rejection. Love does not bow to

popular opinion or approval ratings. Love never
seeks the spotlight or a place at the cool kids' table.
Love is not eager to impress friends or coworkers
with a Pinterest-pretty life. Love does not curry
favor. Love does not demand to be noticed. Love
has eyes that look up, hands that reach out, and
a heart that beats wildly within.

Love never fails.

My Bible's study notes say that this kind of love "is
utterly unselfish. This kind of love goes against our natural
inclinations. It is possible to practice this love only if God
helps us set aside our own desires and instincts, so that we
can give love while expecting nothing in return. Thus the
more we become like Christ, the more love we will show
to others."[5]

Dear God, make us couriers of selfless, Christlike love.

Love compels us to step outside of our own comfort
zones and straight into the heart of Jesus, straight into our
neighborhoods and into all the world. When we begin to
understand the depth of Cross-bought love, our hearts are
turned right-side up. That love changes how we function
at home and in unfamiliar places.

Jesus is asking us the same question He asked Peter on
the beach at the end of the Gospel of John: "Do you love
me more than these?"

We can make a list of all the "these" in our lives: our
comforts, our jobs, our friendships, our reputations. Our

"these" may be good things, but at times, our "these" have overshadowed Thee.

Christ asks us, "Do you love me more than these?" Today, we can answer as Peter did: "Yes, Lord, . . . you know I love you" (John 21:15).

And may it be so every day.

Let's live what we believe, not with passionate words but with passionate lives. We don't need to waste another precious second of this short life worrying about popular opinion. We can live into the real promise of a Cross-shaped love, not the lie of the Love Idol. If we continue to live life *for* our own approval—in a mad chase for worldly significance—we will never truly live *from* our approval. Instead of feasting on Living Bread, we will be filling our bellies with metaphorical mud pies.

This is the trip, in fact, where I first saw those depressing mud pies. We were delivering Bibles and backpacks to the children whom we sponsor from the Touch of Hope school. One of our Haitian friends, Webert, pointed them out as we walked through a village. There were hundreds of them, drying on mats. People in Haiti eat the mud pies because they offer a false sense of satisfaction.

I have never eaten dirt, not even as a kid. But I've consumed a lot of metaphorical mud pies over the years. Perhaps you have too.

When you uproot the Love Idol, you lose your taste for the dirt that it was planted in.

～ぐ～

On one of our last nights in Haiti, Lydia and I are sitting on the porch of our hosts' house, next to the ocean. Lydia tells me she doesn't want to go home.

"I don't know how to go back, Mom," she says.

I tell her that in one sense, going back might be impossible anyway. We can't undo what has happened inside us. We are changed.

We sit in the silence, hundreds of miles from our comfortable life in Iowa, but especially close to our Christ in us. Her skirted legs and dirty feet stretch out next to mine on this seaside porch.

We watch the sun sink into that thin line where ocean touches sky. Across the bay, sparse lights begin to illuminate the Port-au-Prince hillside. The nearly full moon peeks its round face over our village—a reminder that even in the darkest places, we're never without light.

In the long shadows behind us, a Haitian boy sings a song, repeating a single word in Haitian Creole that crosses every language barrier: *A-le-lou-ya*. He sings it over and over again, in this place where life is a hardscrabble fight for survival, where villages are all bone and sagging skin. This is Haiti: the land of the bare feet, the swollen belly, and the persistent Alelouya.

My daughter exhales a long sigh and holds up the book she's been reading while we've been here. She shakes the book in the air, like a banner. It's *Kisses from Katie*,

the story of Katie Davis and her ministry to children
in Uganda.

"Katie says that Jesus wrecked her life," Lydia tells me.
"God turned everything upside down, and later she realized
He actually turned it right-side up."

I wonder where Lydia might be heading with this conversation. The most human part of me—the part I call
"mother"—is scared to know. What if Lydia or Anna won't
go to college because she feels called to Africa? What if my
girls think the only way to serve God is by moving to a
third-world country? Or this: What if I try to sway them
from serving where God calls because I'm more concerned
about their 401(k) plans and convenient access to my
future grandchildren than about His will for their lives?

I know my default response to such things. I've been
on a journey to fight against it, but I know how I can get.

Then again, this is what my husband and I prayed for
before we brought our two daughters to Haiti. Our prayers
have been answered. Because, like Katie, we've all experienced our own beautiful wrecking.

But unlike Katie, we aren't staying in the third world.
Our family of four will soon return home. We will go back
to five brands of cereal on the shelf, a full freezer, iGadgetry,
report cards, work assignments, job evaluations, farm chores,
standards, benchmarks, the American cultural ideal, and the
daily threats unleashed by the Love Idol.

On the porch, I shake my head. Like Lydia, I don't
know how to go back either. I want us to keep our dirty

feet. I suppose, in some ways, we will. Because our two daughters can't un-see what they saw in the orphanages and school yard. They can't un-feel the hands of the orphans or the tight hugs of Haitian sisters. Lydia can't un-read Katie's words or unravel whatever God is weaving in her hungering heart.

The haze of years might blur some of the details, but our daughters have already been changed. When we were walking through the villages a day earlier, Anna told me that she preferred Haiti to Disney, a trip we had taken twice with the girls.

And I can sense the change in Lydia, too, on this sunset night, on the shore of the poorest country in the Western Hemisphere.

Lydia hurls her words into the dusk, like a prayer. "Mom, I don't want to live an average life."

She's only a child, but she finds the right words to wrap around her middle-aged mother's heart. I don't want average either. I want to fight the comfortable middle and the future threat of idols.

I am not sure either of us can articulate what our aspirations might mean for our family.

We really do have to go back to Iowa in two days, but I know this much: We don't have to go back to average. Sure, we've got average moments ahead of us—at the kitchen sink, at the farm gate, in the girls' school classrooms. But I tell Lydia that any average moment in this life is never really average if we're living each ordinary moment for an extraordinary God. And who knows? Maybe our not-so-average lives will bring us back to Haiti someday.

For now we'll sit on the seashore a bit longer, memorizing this moment, while Katie's book sits, with its spine gleaming in the moonlight, and the city lights across the bay shine stubbornly into the dark.

And I hear it again now: the echoing praise of the boy with his Alelouya.

Why is it that when you're busy loving others,
the Love Idol loses its grip on you?

CHAPTER 13

APELLES

This is my command: Love each other.

JESUS CHRIST (JOHN 15:17)

It is Ash Wednesday, the night when mortals remember how temporary we are.

Under the steeple of our country church, Pastor Rich will smear an ashen cross on every forehead in the room, while delivering a thundering reminder to each soul: "To dust you shall return."

Tonight my husband and I serve as church greeters, shaking hands with old friends. Our Haiti-made tans have long since faded. If we stood too long in the frigid freeze of this Midwestern winter night, we could end up with frost-bitten fingertips.

The church's glass doors swing open for wrinkled farm-ers and schoolteachers and mothers with preschoolers zippered against the cold. Old men stamp snowy shoes onto the church's entryway rug. We greet one another, rosy-faced and shivering, by the coatracks with clinking hangers tossed by the wind every time the doors open. My mother-in-law, Joyce, plays her prelude, "Just as I Am," on the church piano.

Old Helmer's blue plastic comb is sticking out of his front shirt pocket. The twice-widowed farmer shakes my hand and then shuffles past our family, finding a seat next to his sister, Hazel, who never married. She's ninety.

Milo tips his hat our way—"Evenin'," he says—then sets his cap on the shelf above all of our coats. He slicks down his silvery-white hair with an open palm. He and his wife, Wanda, find their place in a pew on the north side of the aisle, where they've sat for decades.

Three of my Sunday school students, wearing grape-juice mustaches, scurry past me. I discover that they have taped a "Kick Me" sign to the back side of my sweater. When they peek around the corner by the guest book, I narrow my eyes, point an accusing finger, and shoot them a wry smirk of revenge. They retreat, giggling.

These are my people, spanning almost a whole century of ages. Young or old, one common trait unites us: We're all terminal. On the big screen of eternity's theater, our lives are microscopic blips. "Seventy years are given to us! Some even live to eighty. But even the best years are filled with pain and trouble; soon they disappear, and we fly away" (Psalm 90:10).

I want my wee little blip on the screen to blink boldly for a King, before it flickers out and I fly away.

Tonight, our church family gathers in long, polished-wood rows to remember our fleeting lives. We will be summoned forward to the altar to receive ashes, an ancient tradition to remind us of our mortality. Depressing, perhaps, to ponder death so severely, especially with the exuberant joy of Easter waiting for us on the other side of these forty days of Lent. Depressing, yes. But wholly necessary. Death has a way of distinguishing between the things that are important and the things that aren't. Thus, this night—the somber beginning of a Lenten journey toward a cross and resurrection.

Beneath the wooden cross nailed to the front wall, we will also remember that—mortal and sinful as we are—we belong to a Savior who already loves us. It's a love that, paradoxically, is the gravest and fairest known to man.

We nailed love to a tree—all of us. This radical Cross-bought love is the one message strategically designed by Holy God to change the whole world, and it is ours to share.

God commissioned us. We are the message carriers—the broken and bruised ones, the wrinkled and joyful ones, the healed and forgiven ones. We gather in church sanctuaries around the globe on Wednesday nights and Sunday mornings, and then we are shooed out the door into our mission field, which is most accurately defined as the place right under our feet. The privilege of sharing God's love belongs to the old men with blue combs, the mothers with bundled-up toddlers, and the middle-aged greeters at the glass doors. The privilege belongs to any of us who believe the glorious reality of a love finished fully on Good Friday.

I finally believe the stunning truth about God's love for us—heart-deep. I believe! And I want my itty-bitty blip on heaven's screen to reflect it.

I take a mental snapshot, freeze-framing this Ash Wednesday night in a dimly lit sanctuary. A child lights the altar candles. Along the church walls are brassy plates and wooden plaques etched with the names of our church's dearly departed. When we gather in this holy house, we are a small limb of an enormous family tree, planted on Calvary. Each generation's holy lineage stretches like branches across time and around the planet.

Statistically speaking, more than two billion Christians are alive today. That's about one-third of the global population. This sprawling family has the capacity to change the world with love. We could recalibrate every barometer and approval-o-meter known to man. We have the means, through Christ's Spirit indwelt, to let people know that they are wildly adored and deeply cherished by the King. This sacred assignment to spread love is the privilege of those of us who've smashed the Love Idol.

God is madly in love with us. That's the startling truth. And it would be criminal to keep the news secret.

We, the changed ones, are now the change agents. And out in the great big world, we can find millions upon millions of people who feel kicked down—the unloved, the unapproved, the rejected, the laid off, the abused, the left out, and the mocked. They just want to know they matter in this life to Someone bigger than themselves. And these hungry friends are everywhere.

Look down your favorite pew, and there she is.

Enter us. We're the ones who now know we're *already* loved by this irresistible God, right in the middle of our messes. Let's go love the rest of the people, in Jesus' name.

With God's love on the *inside* of us, we are equipped to unconditionally love people right *beside* us. When we look and love *up*, we can look and love *out*.

I have vowed that my life will be different now that I have begun to embrace real love. God knows that I've botched up some things in the past, thanks to my disordered priorities. God knows I still do.

But who knows how much time I have left? I don't want to waste a millisecond. Life is vapor short (see James 4:14, NKJV). The pastor's ash-tipped forefinger will alert us to such brevity on this night at the altar, in a church tucked among the bare, frozen farm fields of Iowa.

We can start small, really. And together we can be big. Worldwide big.

Because we can start wherever we are, all two billion of us in one gigantic love revolution.

You and I could start in our own backyards and post offices and gymnasium bleachers. The hurting and broken people live next door. You don't have to go to Haiti or Ghana, but you might. You could start today in your own church. You could reach down the pew to squeeze the hand of a friend. I really believe it's that simple. Some of our very own sisters are pretending, quite convincingly, that things are "fine, just fine." But they need your hands, squeezing their hands, to let them know that they don't have to pretend anymore.

More than ever before, the reporter in me wants to broadcast this news—the Good News! Extra, extra, read all about Him. Let the headlines of my life declare the Good News: "You are loved! Already!"

Sure, this life-rattling message of gospel love is intended for the unbelieving two-thirds of the world. But professing Christians need to relearn the love-saturated gospel too. The people holding laser-printed church bulletins in their hands are among the hungriest of the love-starved: emaciated souls trying to get their fill at the world's buffet of flimsy praise. We Christians sing of God's love beneath wooden crosses on Sundays, but we go looking for love and approval in all the wrong places the other six days of the week. I'm the poster child for that problem. That's why I have to come back to the finished work of the Cross every day, while the Lord is still doing a finishing work in me.

Who in my tiny church might need to be reminded of the Good News, the very best news? Who might be a little bit afraid to show the depth of her own bruised heart?

A popular catchphrase has made the rounds through Christian circles: "Be real and authentic." That's what we say—but do we really mean it? Do we make safe places for people to be real in our faith communities? Do we want to see people's "real"? What about when someone's real is mad at God? When their real is ugly? When their real can't stop crying for days, even weeks? When their real is chronic? Do we want people to be real then?

It can be hard to be real because we're not convinced that people want to see it. It can be painful to let down the facade in Christian circles. I wish it weren't so, because the Christian people are our people. But it's true. I do wonder, how often have we left fellow Christians with the impression that once they're saved, they ought to get their act together and keep it that way?

I've overheard, on occasion, women whispering about their Christian sisters' unkempt children, unclean kitchens, too-long grass, spotty church attendance, moodiness. All of that stings. We tell each other that it's safe to be authentic, but are we making nonthreatening places for people to be less than perfect?

I've seen how women have felt rejected because they didn't "fix" quickly enough. Their marriages got rockier instead of better. Their children ended up with DUIs instead of 401(k)s. They fell from the grace of people, from the approval of their peers.

But they never fell from the heart of God.

I want to go where Jesus goes—straight back to the cross, where the grace-clingers dwell. I want to let people know that they matter to God, they matter to others, and they matter to me. Not because of the size of their jeans, their bank accounts, or their influence, but simply because of the size of their God.

Oh, God, let us love people like You do. Show us how. Show Your daughters how to better love those who are out of sync, out of fashion, and out of our own cliques. Don't let us treat our wounded sisters as short-term charity projects but as long-term friends.

Standing at the back of the sanctuary, I scan the room to see the heads bowed. How precious are these souls in the pews—mothers popping oat circles into pink little mouths, opened like the beaks of baby birds. Factory workers and insurance men and adolescent dreamers staring into the middle-distance. The jobless and worried and widows, still grieving. From my vantage point at the back of the church, I see the "nobodies," the unnoticed wallflowers, hunched in pews right behind the "somebodies," who are living at the top of their game. And all of them are loved wildly, no more or no less than the guy two feet away.

The ground is, as they say, level at the foot of the cross. God loves us all the same. He died for us all the same.

Empowered, we could be part of a worldwide ministry of radical love, if we dared. The future is in our very hands.

The same is true of you: God loves you, and He likes you. And He is calling you to love others.

Broken as you and I are, we are the carriers of Christ's love to a world in need.

Let's not miss the opportunity.

It is 6:59 p.m. on Ash Wednesday. Art Stensland rises from his pew to ring the bell, which has been modernized with a control switch on the back wall. He waits, with his hand on the switch.

At the front of the church, Pastor Rich nods his head, the cue for Art to ring the bell.

And with the flip of a wall switch—*thwock*—Our Savior's church bell rings over the fields.

My husband, Scott, has found an open pew for us behind Helmer and Hazel. Hazel sits with her head bowed, a crown of white. Her fingers, knotted like oak twigs, are folded on her lap.

A few days ago, I asked Hazel if she had advice for women like us. So she invited me over. I sat down with her in her unassuming, squarish farmhouse down the gravel road from our home. I was hungry for wisdom. She gave me some, along with a butter cookie on a cracked china plate.

I figured that Hazel, who has never been a bride to anyone but Christ, must have this whole approval thing licked.

As long as I've known her, she has lived a quiet, unrushed existence in a house that hasn't undergone a remodel in approximately forever. I asked her that afternoon if she'd ever heard of Facebook or Pinterest—these modern-day hangouts where people are tempted to preen, compare, and approval seek—and she laughed a hearty laugh that made her chin wobble. I told her about Twitter, and she slapped her knee, saying birds—not people—are the ones God made to tweet.

So it stunned me when she told me that she, too, had struggled at times with comparison and jealousy. She had wanted a cuter hairstyle, a cleaner house, the right words so her out-loud prayers didn't sound garbled at Ladies' Aid.

She was not on the "be real" bandwagon by choice, but God placed her there despite her protests.

"I relate to the woman who needed healing in Mark 5," Hazel told me over glasses of lemonade. "If I could have touched the hem of Jesus' garment secretly, I would have. But Jesus didn't let that woman get by with that. And He won't let us get away with it either."

As the years have passed, bringing Hazel closer to the day she will see her only Groom face-to-face, "the things of this world have grown strangely dim." "As I grow older, He has become more and more precious to me," she said.

We talked that day about Hazel's favorite Bible verses and her favorite hymns—"Just as I Am" among them. She told me that when she leaves earth, she wants people to know that she was faithful. But even more than that, she wants them to know that *Christ* is faithful.

"I want people to know that Jesus loves them, and that He died for them, and they are loved and forgiven." Her ninety-year-old voice shook when she uttered the simplest truths that we complicate with our performance-driven lives. It really is that uncomplicated: We are already loved and forgiven.

And tonight I find a place right behind Hazel in our church sanctuary, where all of us face a wooden cross, on which our approval was long ago secured with iron spikes.

Apelles knew it. Apelles *lived* it.

In the weeks between Ash Wednesday and the Resurrection, I found his name tucked away in Scripture, like hidden treasure. His name was dropped in among those of others whom Paul greeted before signing off his letter to the Romans. I had never before noticed Apelles. But he's been there always, unpretentiously immortalized in a seven-word greeting in the Bible: "Greet Apelles, tested and approved in Christ" (Romans 16:10, NIV).

That's all that Paul wrote about Apelles. Just one sentence, nothing else. No accolades or applause or records of great conquests.

I highlighted the three words "approved in Christ" in green. My spirit quickened, and my cheeks flushed. These are the words forever etched for Apelles: *approved* in Christ.

My eyes dropped to the bottom of the page, hoping for something more in the study notes, some explanation or a cross-reference so I could find out more about this Christ-approved man. But there was nothing. I opened my computer's Bible software, searching to find Apelles somewhere else in Scripture. Surely, there would be more about a man who earned a mention from Paul. I typed in his name, waited expectantly as I stared at the screen, then . . . nothing.

His name appears once, and only once, in Scripture. This is all Apelles will ever be known for, that he was "approved in Christ." And in the end, it may be all that really matters.

He was not Apelles the Great. He was not Apelles the Hero. No mention of Apelles the Popular, Apelles the Witty, Apelles the Man of the Year, Apelles the Golden Child, Apelles the Valedictorian.

He was Apelles the Approved.

I wonder often about Apelles's earthly life. He may have been the nobody in the back row. Or he might have been a big somebody who preached about Jesus among crowds in Rome. Apelles may have fought the same battle we've been fighting. He may have, at times, been jealous or envious, or wished for a greater mention by key Christian leaders like Paul. Maybe he felt unloved by his parents. He may have fought approval until his last breath. I don't know, of course.

Scripture does not reveal a single act of human bravery or personal accomplishment on his part, unlike his peers whom Paul mentioned. In verse 6, Paul tells us that Mary "worked very hard." In verse 7, Paul introduces us to

Andronicus and Junias, "outstanding among the apostles."
In verse 9, Paul calls Stachys out as a "dear" friend. And in
verse 12, we meet Persis, who "has worked very hard in the
Lord" (Romans 16:6-12, NIV).

How many times had Satan whispered in Apelles's ears,
What will people think of you? How often did Apelles have
to fight the urge to compare himself to his well-known
contemporaries? Did it come easier for Apelles than it does
for us? Was Apelles so secure that he never tried to please
others, to stand out, or to make a name for himself?

I won't know on this side of life. But on the other side
of forever, when I come into glory, I want a lunch date
with Apelles.

Maybe he will tell me that he lived out his days satisfied
that Christ's love and approval were enough. I am sure
Apelles will tell me that, in the end, he had the only stamp
of approval that really mattered.

Pastor Rich instructs us to stand for our opening hymn.
We rise to sing:

> *Beautiful Savior,*
> *King of Creation,*
> *Son of God and Son of Man!*
> *Truly I'd love Thee,*
> *Truly I'd serve Thee,*
> *Light of my soul, my Joy, my Crown.*[1]

I run my finger along the hymnal lyrics so my little Anna can follow the words, lisping through the wide, toothless gap in her mouth. And that last note rings long and loud in my heart: God as my Crown.

The congregation sits.

Our call to worship begins its ascent into the night sky, like a clarion call for Christ. It echoes out across the cemetery, where the rising moon glints off the granite flecks of gravestones, and out over the hibernating fields. For most of us in this hushed sanctuary, the cemetery across the road will be our final resting place. We walk by our very own grave sites every Sunday morning.

At every funeral, Art stands in the back of the sanctuary to sound the bell for the dead. It's a ringing benediction. For a few hours, farmers trade denim for pressed polyester so they can reverently heft caskets across county blacktop K-12. The rest of us pull coats off the clinking hangers, and then cross over that doormat. With Kleenexes in our fists, we follow the procession to gather around gaping rectangles cut into the cemetery ground.

After we turn our backs, the graves are closed.

And within hours, the fresh flowers on our friends' graves wither. In the scope of eternity, so do the memories. Sure, for a season we remember. At church potlucks, we regale one another with stories of her prize-winning apple pie, his hearty laughs, her legendary soprano voice, their contributions to the church and to the community—and perhaps even to the world at large. And believe me, they were amazing. Our world is filled with heroes worth every bold-print headline.

If you're a real somebody, you might even make the history books.

But as the years pass, new heroes' names grace the front pages of newspapers, the playbills on opening night, and the team rosters pinned to the gymnasium wall.

Friend, I hope you do great things with your life. I hope it's big for Jesus and for His people. But my wish for you, and for me, is that we would be content with knowing that our "divine accolade"—as C. S. Lewis calls it—is coming. Even if no one ever approves of who we are, my prayer is that we could be content knowing that Christ longs to speak these words over us: "Well done, my good and faithful servant" (Matthew 25:21).

He is waiting to tell you in person how much He has always loved you.

You are God's favorite. He loves you best, because you are His friend. Greater love has no man than this, that he would lay down his life for a friend (see John 15:13). And Jesus did. For you, whose name coursed though the beating heart of a dying Savior who now lives and reigns in heaven.

In this life, you may never win a popularity contest. You may never win your parents' approval. You may never be in the spotlight. Indeed, the world may actually think you're a nerd or a geek or a loser. But Jesus said, "Keep in mind that it hated me first" (John 15:18, NIV). I guess that puts you in good company, if you find yourself crushed by unrequited love or haunted by the enemy questioning your worth in the world.

Even then, Jesus still loves you best. He has marked you as His bride.

His fathomless love changes how you and I will live in our moments, how we'll love in our neighborhoods, and what we'll be known for in eternity.

I have decided. I want to be about the cause of Jesus. I want to follow Christ, not the crowd. And I will fight for that until the end.

The Ash Wednesday sermon ends, and Pastor Rich calls us forward from the pews. We rise, filling the center aisle. We are one long line of paupers approaching the altar of startling grace.

A hush falls over the room. No music. No whispering. Just the thundering repetition of words as the pastor rubs black crosses onto foreheads: "Remember you are dust, and to dust you shall return."

I shuffle to the front with my family. I once heard someone say that we bring nothing to the altar but our sin. God takes it away, while miraculously avalanching us with His love—just as He has always done.

Before the foundations of the world, He loved you. Before the fall of Eden, He loved you. Before He sent His Son splitting through the cosmos to this world, He loved you. Before He died upon the cross, He loved you. When

He rose again, He loved you. And He's coming back again because He loves you. When you took your first breath, He loved you. When you messed up bad, He loved you. When you made good grades, He loved you. When you won and when you lost, He loved you.

I can feel it here, at the front of my church: He loves me.

I want to love others just like that. I know how incredible it feels to be loved like this, unconditionally, simply because I exist.

The pastor stands in front of me now. He presses a cross onto my skin, the same patch of skin that Rev. Vickery sprinkled with water nearly four decades ago. I close my eyes.

Flecks of ash fall on my nose.

And right here, right where I'm standing, someday they'll set my casket with the lid open. And perhaps someone will set sprays of daisies and carnations around me, with little notes in plastic holders shoved between the blooms, saying I was a devoted mom and wife, a great friend, and a tireless volunteer. They might even use the word *beloved*. Sure, that would be fine.

The bell will toll. Someone will close the lid, sealing it until that last day. And they'll carry my body across the road, with my face toward heaven.

Someone will tap out a few short lines for the obituary page. But by the time those old newspaper presses roll, I'll already be standing before God. Any applause on earth will have long faded from my ears. And I won't even care. I will have come face-to-face with my Savior. And I pray that He will speak those words to me, the highest compliment from the Highest King. I pray that my Savior will take me by the hand and whisper in my ear what my love-hungry heart has always longed to hear, above all other words of affirmation: "Well done, good and faithful servant."

You can say nice things about me if you want when I'm gone. You can say that I wrote some fine news stories, and maybe you found my name along the spine of a book or two. You might find an old award in a rusting filing cabinet, and that might offer some proof that I did such and such, once upon a time.

That would be fine, I suppose, but by then I will have found the reward of greatest price, in the presence of my King.

And there I will have learned at last what it means to live like Apelles, that there is no greater compliment to pay a person than this: You have been approved in Christ.

I hope someone engraves it on my tombstone. And don't pity me the day I die. For on that day, I will have found the approval I always wanted, and I will know right then, with certainty, that it's the approval I always had.

How can you help others in your home, church, or neighborhood stop chasing the empty promises of their Love Idols and rest in God's grace instead?

EPILOGUE

Therefore, since we are surrounded by such a great cloud of
witnesses, let us throw off everything that hinders and the sin
that so easily entangles. And let us run with perseverance the
race marked out for us, fixing our eyes on Jesus, the pioneer
and perfecter of faith. For the joy set before him he endured
the cross, scorning its shame, and sat down at
the right hand of the throne of God.

HEBREWS 12:1-2, NIV

THE CHRISTIAN AND the runner both know this to be true:
In that heart-pounding moment when a finish line comes
gloriously into view, a person's perspective completely
changes.

Someone might credit adrenaline. Another might say it
happens because faith has become sight in one magical
moment. I suspect it's a lot of both.

Until that instant when you see the finish, a race can seem
brutally unforgiving, even endless. As a runner—and as a
human—I have faced merciless headwinds, steep inclines,
and people passing me on both sides. I have wanted, at times,
to give up. But then you turn a corner and find yourself

utterly astonished to discover that you've nearly made it. In the twinkling of an eye, every ache fades from memory. The finish is so close you can taste it. You're not sure whether to weep or laugh or fall to your knees. But suddenly you find yourself running like mad to get there.

Right then, you realize you were made for a moment like this.

That's how it happened for Lydia and me on a warm June morning. We had gone to my hometown—Marathon, Iowa—to run a 5K side by side. Numbers 566 and 567 were pinned to the fronts of our shirts. Lydia and I were a few hundred feet from the finish line, and she was exhausted. Honestly, she was moments away from giving up entirely.

But then we turned by the old brick post office on Main Street, where Mom and Dad collected their mail from PO Box 5 for more than four decades.

When Lydia and I rounded that corner, our chests heaving, we could both see a long, white banner flapping over a spray-painted line on the street. The finish line stretched between the old brick church, where I was baptized and confirmed, and the empty lot where the schoolhouse once stood—the school where Mrs. Huseman told me, "There always will be tomorrow."

In that moment, I felt like I could stretch out a hand and touch tomorrow.

"Look, Lydia!" I managed between breaths. "Look! See there? . . . We're really . . . going to . . . make it!"

In that split second, Lydia's weariness magically lifted.

And suddenly the two of us felt weightless, like we were suspended in air, like our soles were three feet above the street, like we could fly.

I grabbed for Lydia's hand and squeezed it.

"I'm so proud of you, honey!" I said it with tears burning my eyes. "You did it!"

"I'm proud . . . of you, too, . . . Mommy!"

Lydia's hand returned the squeeze. Her pace quickened, propelled by a burst of inner moxie.

A smile stretched across her face like a sunrise. Lydia had completely forgotten that, minutes earlier, she didn't think she could take another step. Everything hurt. We were at the back of a thinning pack.

We knew we would be among the last to cross the finish line.

But now, the end was in view. Nothing else mattered. It didn't matter that we'd been passed by almost everyone else, that records had been shattered, that the loudest applause had already been offered, or that all the medals were hanging around other necks.

This was *our* race.

The finish line is an equal-opportunity destination. It's a place that beckons the best and the brightest, the gasping and the gawky, the winners and the losers. Every soul who dares set out on this course of life in Christ has been given rights to cross over when her race is done. And every person who crosses the finish line longs for that moment when she'll hear her name called out.

That morning in Marathon, I was granted a small foretaste of how beautiful our heavenly finish will be. As Lydia and I neared the end of our race, we could see a man at the finish line, standing on a flatbed trailer with a microphone.

That man was my father.

For years, Dad has presided over this finish line, welcoming thousands of breathless runners. They cross the line after completing 5Ks, marathons, and half marathons in my hometown's annual Marathon to Marathon event.

Some of the runners show up with arms raised, pumping victorious fists into the air. Others stumble across. Many cry. A few fall to their knees. But no matter how they get there, Dad always wants the runners to hear their names called out over the loudspeaker.

"There's something to be said for hearing your name called out, after you've worked so hard, trained so long, and come so far," Dad told me once. "I will never leave the finish line until the last person has crossed over, and I don't care how long it takes, because I want every person to hear their name."

Lydia and I couldn't wait to hear ours. And now we were seconds away.

Dad was looking right at Lydia and me, and I don't think I was imagining the sparkle in his eye. He was so proud of us.

Dad lifted the microphone and called out the words that Lydia had longed to hear. "Way to go, Lydia Lee! You made it!" The crowd cheered for that fierce little runner.

Then I heard my father's words for me:

"And that's my daughter, Jennifer!"

And I suppose the crowd was applauding for me too.
I can't be sure. All I remember were the words my father
saved just for me, his daughter. I remember the welcome of
a father who loves me and was waiting for me, a father who
was pleased with me despite my performance. And I knew
in that moment, when he called his daughter across the
line, that the best words we can ever hear will come at
the finish.

Friend, there really is a finish line.

There really is a great crowd of witnesses, waiting. You
can't see them, but they are already cheering for you.

There really is a Father, waiting to welcome you.

And, sister, it really is all because of Jesus that you're
running in the first place.

You may still be toward the beginning of your story,
this long narrative that stretches out into forever. And
I'm reaching out my hands to you right now, putting
one on each shoulder, because I want to tell you something: I believe in you. I believe you're going to make it.
I believe in you because I believe in Jesus. He has a race
marked out for you. And He will run alongside you until
the last light of your life fades. You can never outrun
Jesus. And Jesus' love will never, ever run out. It might
take the whole rest of your life before you know that truth
in all its magnificent fullness. The good Lord might well
have to remind you right up until that moment when you

step over the finish line, because the world will continue to make a grab for you. You will face headwinds and steep inclines. You might feel like a nobody, the last one on the track, long forgotten. You might want something—or someone—you can never have.

But you will finish. And Jesus will be waiting.

I don't think that Jesus will mind if I speak for Him here, to tell you one more time that He already loves you.

With God's grace, you and I will keep our eyes fixed on the destination ahead, rather than on the sidelines at whoever might be watching. He has words for us at the finish that will drown out every ounce of approval we ever sought here on earth.

And when that glorious finish line comes into view, we will run like mad, and the wind will whip through our hair, and we'll forget how bad it hurt sometimes. Because we can't wait to cross over and hear the words we were created to hear at the finish: "Well done, good and faithful servant."

And just think: that grand moment will not be the end. We will have only just begun.

The Love Idol Movement

Visit www.loveidolbook.com to join a
community of women who are smashing
their Love Idols. Download your FREE
printable from the site to identify where the
love idols may be lurking in your life.
Then celebrate your freedom online with a
movement of women who are reclaiming
their "preapproved" identity in Christ.

**Join the #loveidol movement on Twitter,
Facebook, and Instagram**

Endnotes

INTRODUCTION: THE *WHAT* IDOL?

1. 1 Corinthians 13:13, NIV

CHAPTER 2: CLOUT

1. James Truslow Adams, *The Epic of America* (Boston: Little, Brown, 1933), 415. As quoted in David Platt's *Radical: Taking Back Your Faith from the American Dream* (Colorado Springs: Multnomah, 2010), 45–46.
2. "About David Yepsen," *Paul Simon Public Policy Institute*, http://paulsimon institute.org/index.php?option=com_content&view=article&id=236&Ite mid=304.

CHAPTER 3: CONVICTION

1. Philippians 3:8
2. Jennifer Dukes Lee, "McVeigh faces last day," Main News, *Des Moines Register*, June 11, 2001, 1.
3. Mother Teresa, *Come Be My Light: The Private Writings of the Saint of Calcutta* (New York: Random House, 2007).
4. Exodus 32:4, NIV
5. Blaise Pascal, *Pensées* (New York: E. P. Dutton, 1958), 113.
6. See Romans 5:8.
7. Lee, "McVeigh faces last day," 1.
8. Ibid.
9. William Ernest Henley, "Invictus," lines 15–16.

CHAPTER 4: MUD PIES

1. Max Lucado says something similar: "I believe Satan trains battalions of demons to whisper one question in our ears: 'What are people thinking of you?'" See *It's Not about Me* (Nashville: Thomas Nelson, 2004), 92.
2. Much-Afraid is the main character in *Hinds' Feet on High Places*, an allegorical novel by Hannah Hurnard written in 1955.

CHAPTER 5: BEE STING

1. A. W. Tozer, *The Pursuit of God* (Camp Hill, PA: WingSpread Publishers, 2007), 42.

CHAPTER 6: "GOD'S GOT IT"

1. Beth Moore, *So Long, Insecurity: You've Been a Bad Friend to Us* (Carol Stream, IL: Tyndale, 2010), xiii.
2. Madeleine L'Engle, *A Circle of Quiet* (New York: HarperCollins, 1972), 28.
3. Madeleine L'Engle, *A Wrinkle in Time* (New York: Square Fish, 2007), 114.
4. "Now faith is being sure of what we hope for and certain of what we do not see" (Hebrews 11:1, NIV 1984).
5. C. S. Lewis, *The Weight of Glory* (New York: HarperCollins, 2009), 36.

CHAPTER 7: "DO YOU WANT TO GET WELL?"

1. Study note for John 5:6, *The Life Application Study Bible*.
2. Moore, *So Long, Insecurity*, 4.
3. A. W. Tozer, "Faith Dares to Fail," ch. 7 in *The Best of A. W. Tozer, Book 1*, comp. Warren Wiersbe (Camp Hill, PA: WingSpread Publishers, 2007).

CHAPTER 8: PREAPPROVED

1. Jerry Bridges, *The Discipline of Grace: God's Role and Our Role in the Pursuit of Holiness* (Colorado Springs: NavPress, 1994), 26.
2. Brennan Manning, *The Ragamuffin Gospel: Good News for the Bedraggled, Beat-Up, and Burnt Out* (Colorado Springs: Multnomah, 2005), 86.
3. Thomas Chalmers, *The Expulsive Power of a New Affection* (Minneapolis: Curiosmith, 2012), 19. Originally published in 1855 by Thomas Constable and Co., Edinburgh.
4. Timothy Keller, *Counterfeit Gods: The Empty Promises of Money, Sex, and Power, and the Only Hope That Matters* (New York: Penguin, 2009), 45, emphasis mine.
5. Tullian Tchividjian, *Jesus + Nothing = Everything* (Wheaton, IL: Crossway, 2011), 22. Emphasis in original.
6. Ibid., 24. Emphasis in original.
7. Ibid., 73. Emphasis in original.

CHAPTER 9: VERY LITTLE

1. Stephen Manes, *Be a Perfect Person in Just Three Days* (New York: Yearling, 1996; 1982), 71–72.
2. Amy Carmichael, *If* (Fort Washington, PA: CLC Publications, 2011), 43. Copyright 1938 by The Donhavur Fellowship. Originally published by SPCK London, 1938.
3. Henri J. M. Nouwen, *The Return of the Prodigal Son: A Story of Homecoming* (New York: Doubleday, 1992), 42. Emphasis in original.
4. C. S. Lewis, *The Four Loves* (New York: Mariner Books, 1971), 65. Originally published by Harcourt, 1960.
5. John Calvin, *Institutes of the Christian Religion* (Peabody, MA: Hendrickson Publishers, 2008), 17.
6. Keller, *Counterfeit Gods*, xviii.
7. James MacDonald, "Freedom from People Pleasing Part 1," podcast audio, *Walk in the Word*, May 9, 2012, www.oneplace.com/ministries/walk-in-the-word/player/freedom-from-people-pleasing-part-1-278908.html.
8. Tchividjian, *Jesus + Nothing = Everything*, 91–92.
9. John Piper, "Battling the Unbelief of a Haughty Spirit," podcast audio, December 18, 1988, www.desiringgod.org/resource-library/sermons/battling-the-unbelief-of-a-haughty-spirit.

CHAPTER 10: CUPPED HANDS

1. Helen H. Lemmel, "Turn Your Eyes upon Jesus," 1922, lines 5–8.
2. Emphasis in quotation mine. Charles Spurgeon, "Christ's Yoke and Burden," *SpurgeonGems.org*, no. 2832 (September 2, 1886): 4. http://spurgeongems.org/vols49-51/chs2832.pdf.
3. Spurgeon, "Christ's Yoke and Burden," 5.
4. Timothy Keller, *The Freedom of Self-Forgetfulness: The Path to True Christian Joy* (Chorley, England: 10Publishing, 2012), 32–33. To read Keller's definition of humility, see *The Meaning of Marriage* (New York: Dutton, 2011), 58.
5. Keller, *The Freedom of Self-Forgetfulness*, 42.

CHAPTER 12: HAITIAN HALLELUJAH

1. Touch of Hope is a nonprofit organization founded in 2011 when the Grooters family of Rock Rapids, Iowa, partnered with local teacher Webert Raymond of Simonette, Haiti. Together, Raymond and the Grooters built a school that now educates more than seven hundred children and provides jobs in the Simonette area. Vi Bella Jewelry (www.ViBellaJewelry.com) impacts the lives of at-risk women in Haiti, Mexico, and the United States by creating jobs that pay good wages and provide a safe working environment. The women

serve as artists "up-cycling" discarded plastic and glass bottles by transforming them into handmade jewelry. All profits are invested back into the artists' communities. The job-creation ministry was founded after fellow Iowan Julie Hulstein visited Haiti in 2010.

2. Oswald Chambers, *My Utmost for His Highest* (Grand Rapids, MI: Discovery House Publishers, 1992), 5.

3. Maura R. O'Connor, "Two Years Later, Haitian Earthquake Death Toll in Dispute," *Columbia Journalism Review*, January 12, 2012, www.cjr.org/behind _the_news/one_year_later_haitian_earthqu.php?page=all.

4. Katie Davis of Brentwood, Tennessee, visited Uganda in 2006. She was captivated by the country and felt burdened to do something for its many impoverished, uneducated children. She returned to Uganda the next year and later established a nonprofit organization called Amazima Ministries International. She is now the mother of thirteen Ugandan daughters. Christine Caine is an activist, pastor, and evangelist who founded the A21 Campaign to fight modern-day human trafficking.

5. Study notes for 1 Corinthians 13:4-7, *The Life Application Study Bible*.

CHAPTER 13: APELLES

1. Author Unknown, "Beautiful Savior," translated by Joseph A. Seiss, 1873.

Discussion Guide

Dearest Friends,

My prayer is that the study guide on the following pages will serve as your road map as you journey through Love Idol. I pray that this guide will help you apply my story and insights to your beautiful, God-adored hearts.

This guide is designed for a four-week study of Love Idol. The questions were created for you to use in group or individual reflection. Feel free to adjust for a shorter or longer study. Let the Holy Spirit lead you.

I've included prayers at the end of each week's study session, which you can read aloud as a group at the end of each session. Feel free to personalize the prayers, or pray the words that God puts on your hearts.

This discussion guide is a place where we can begin to get honest with ourselves, to dig deep, and to unearth the Love Idols that have been lurking in our lives.

I pray that you and I will continue to discover the depths of God's love for us in our journeys. I pray that we will know, for certain, that the approval we've always been longing for is the approval that's already ours.

One of His beloved,

Jennifer

Week 1: Reaching Back

This week, let's look back. Together, we will explore our pasts to pinpoint places where the Love Idol has gained a foothold in our lives.

Read the introduction and chapters 1 through 3

INTRODUCTION: THE *WHAT* IDOL?

1. Have you ever thought about love being an idol? It might sound a bit absurd. But it's true: some of God's greatest gifts, like love, can be twisted into idols. Have you ever sought the gifts of love and approval more ardently than you've sought the Giver Himself? How so?

2. Can you identify places in your life where you've desired another's love or approval in a way that might be unhealthy? Explain.

3. The Love Idol can manifest itself in a variety of ways: perfectionism, approval seeking, people pleasing, comparing ourselves to others. Which do you most relate to?

4. When was the last time you heard the enemy whisper this question in your ear: "What will people think of you?" How did you react?

CHAPTER 1: PICTURE PERFECT

1. Many of us have felt enslaved to our performances. We have been pressured—or perhaps have pressured ourselves—to excel in school, on the job, in our families of origin, even in

our churches. Describe one or more times early in life when you felt you needed to "perform" to win the love or approval of people in your life.

2. Paul wrote: "Our purpose is to please God, not people" (1 Thessalonians 2:4). But the truth is, we don't always want to please God. We actually *like* pleasing people. Why do you suppose we prefer people's approval over God's approval, when Scripture so clearly identifies this as a misguided desire and a sin?

CHAPTER 2: CLOUT

1. Flip through the photo album of your own life. Where do you see the Love Idol lurking in your grade school years? Your high school years? Your early adulthood? This past week?

2. Often the Love Idol makes us live in fear that we'll mess up while people are watching. We wear a false confidence, fearing that our peers or coworkers will discover the flawed versions of ourselves. Have you ever feared that the facade might drop and you might be "found out"? What did you do to hide the real version of yourself?

CHAPTER 3: CONVICTION

1. Read Exodus 32:1-4. How can you apply the story about the golden calf to a time in your life when you fashioned an idol out of love—a love that you could see and feel and touch? Whose love or approval were you seeking?

2. Why are we tempted to manufacture a Love Idol when God's presence isn't immediately obvious to us?

3. Compliments and praise are great, in healthy doses. But how often have you *craved* affirmation? When was the last time you were deflated by a lack of praise?

4. Can you describe a situation in which the Love Idol delivered short-term satisfaction? In what ways did it fail to satisfy your long-term needs?

Dear God, it's not easy to peek behind the curtain and face my personal history. It's not easy to see how I have fallen into traps and temptations. Yet I know that when I get honest with myself, I am also getting honest with You. I can't slay the Love Idols in my life without You. So I'm trusting You to walk with me. Help me do battle against the idols that have been strangling my heart. And, Lord, as I think about my past and present mistakes, guard my heart and mind. The enemy would love nothing more than for my journey toward freedom from the Love Idol to stop right now. Help me persevere, through the power of Your Holy Spirit. Amen.

Week 2: Reaching In

Last week, we spent most of our time reaching back into our past to see where the Love Idol has lurked. This week, let's take an honest look inward, as we begin to slay the idol that has long gripped our hearts.

Read chapters 4 through 7

CHAPTER 4: MUD PIES

1. Have you ever felt like a change of address—a move out of a relationship, out of a church, or out of a neighborhood—would solve your innermost problems? Share an example. Sometimes such moves are necessary for our spiritual and emotional well-being. But why isn't a physical move a cure-all?

2. In 2 Timothy 2:15, Paul writes: "Work hard so you can present yourself to God and receive his approval"—*not* so we can present ourselves to our peers or spouses or pastor or neighbors. We are called to present ourselves to God and receive His approval. In your own life, to whom have you tried to "present yourself"?

3. Consider the mud pie analogy on pages 56–57. In an effort to feel fulfilled, what "mud pies" have you consumed, only to be left hungry again?

CHAPTER 5: BEE STING

1. Do you agree that sin is at the root of approval seeking? Why or why not?

2. Lydia Lee stepped onto the spelling bee stage, despite her fears. She risked failing for the sheer joy of trying. When have you stopped short of trying something new because you feared failing while someone was watching?

3. If your Love Idol demands that you perform to high standards, could you dare yourself to "get a B" today—whether on an actual assignment or as you try living up to the expectations of those around you? What is the worst thing that could happen if you got a B, or even an F?

CHAPTER 6: "GOD'S GOT IT"

1. We know how the Love Idol stands in the way of our spiritual health. But the idol can also throw itself between you and God's call on your life. In what ways might the Love Idol be trying to block the way to your Kingdom calling?

2. Name one concrete action you could take in the next week to step straight into your fear, straight over your self-doubts, and straight into God's purposes for you.

3. The apostle Paul asks, "Am I now trying to win the approval of human beings, or of God? Or am I trying to please people?" (Galatians 1:10, NIV). How would you answer his questions?

CHAPTER 7: "DO YOU WANT TO GET WELL?"

1. My pastor friend said the "cure is the process," meaning that throughout life, we may have to continue battling old compulsions. Do you agree or disagree? Explain.

2. Read the story of the woman who needed healing in Luke 8:43-48. In verse 45, why do you think Jesus asked, "Who touched me?" Pause for a moment to listen for His voice in your spirit. What is He asking you?

3. Receiving positive affirmation and validation is actually a good thing. We were designed by God to love and be loved. When do you think healthy validation crosses the line and becomes an idol?

4. Jesus once asked a crippled man, "Do you want to get well?" (John 5:6, NIV). Do you want to get well? If you feel you can, answer Jesus' question out loud for yourself.

   Dear Jesus, I really do want to get well. I want to let go of any notions about love and approval that don't line up with the gospel. This is me: letting go. I am calling out my problem by its actual name, and when I name it, I'm one step closer to canceling its power. Thank You, Lord, for helping me name this idol that has gripped my heart for too long. Now, help me to uproot it. This idol has taken up space that belongs only to You. I give those places back to You and ask You to fill me with Your love and approval. I need You. Amen.

Week 3: Reaching Up

In Week 1, we reached back into our past. Last week, we made an honest assessment of our inward lives, as they exist right now. This week, we gratefully rejoice as we reach a hand up to find the hand of Christ reaching down to us.

Read chapters 8 through 10

CHAPTER 8: PREAPPROVED

1. If you're already a Christian, why would you need to continue to evangelize yourself with the gospel? How can you practically do that in your day-to-day life?

2. Do you agree that the church is full of approval-hungry people, sitting in the pews and maybe standing at the pulpits? If so, why do you think that is?

3. Look around you. How is God whispering the truest love language into your life and your world? Keep a list this week of God's love notes, as a reminder of all the ways you're valued by the King.

4. Be on the lookout for that one word—approved—written on credit-card offers and receipts. At last, you have a reason to celebrate "junk mail"! What have you learned about the way God sees you after reading the first eight chapters of this book?

CHAPTER 9: VERY LITTLE

1. God is the embodiment of love (1 John 4:8). Love is God's character toward us. How might that knowledge change how you view your own worth?

2. Paul, the former approval seeker, wrote that the opinion of others was "a very little" thing. (See 1 Corinthians 4:3.) What do you need to make "very little" today?

3. If we're secure in our Christ identity, we'll be able to live more fully. How risky does it feel to wear the Real You on the outside, instead of tucking the most honest version of yourself away somewhere "safe"?

CHAPTER 10: CUPPED HANDS

1. Old insecurities like to make unannounced visits. What can you do to remind yourself of your true identity, especially in the moments when your flesh wants you to return to old patterns of seeking approval from people?

2. Timothy Keller writes: "True gospel-humility means I stop connecting every experience, every conversation, with myself. In fact, I stop thinking about myself. . . . A truly gospel-humble person is not a self-hating person or a self-loving person, but a gospel-humble person" (see page 170). How can you apply Keller's assertion in your own life?

3. When we are focused on the Wow Factor of God, we are less inclined to try to impress or wow others. How has God wowed you this week?

4. The enemy can't stand the praise and adoration of God. Go ahead—boast about the goodness of God and send Satan packing.

Gracious and loving God, today I say, "Alleluia, what a Savior!" Thank You for a love that is already mine. I don't have to earn anyone's love or attention; I can turn around and receive Cross-bought love, freely given. I don't have anything to prove. In You, I'm preapproved. At times, my rebel heart may falter. The world's ways will woo. The Love Idol may stage a comeback. Help me, Lord, to evict the Love Idol every day with the gospel truth about who I am in You. Help me to seek Christ-esteem over self-esteem until I take my last breath. In Jesus' name, Amen.

Week 4: Reaching Out

In Week 1, we reviewed our past. In Week 2, we explored our inward lives. Last week, God reminded us that we are loved—preapproved!—not because of our performance, but because of His Son. This week, we will reach out to others and love our neighbor as Christ commanded.

Read chapters 11 through 13 and the epilogue

CHAPTER 11: BLEACHERS

1. God has a habit of making a name for Himself through the feeble and frail. Jesus told Paul, "My power works best in weakness" (2 Corinthians 12:9-10). How can that truth about your own weakness change the way you live today?

2. A person who has evicted the Love Idol is no longer envious of others who are in the spotlight. How can this literal change of heart free a person to genuinely appreciate the accomplishments of others? Whom can you celebrate today with a word of encouragement?

3. Consider the next time you'll have the opportunity to pray the Patty Prayer: "Dear God, let my words and my life honor You. I'm willing to fall flat on my face if it brings glory to You. In Jesus' name, Amen." How do you feel as you consider praying it? Would you be willing to laugh at yourself if you actually *do* trip on the hem of your pants as I did?

CHAPTER 12: HAITIAN HALLELUJAH

1. Scripture tells us to love our neighbors as ourselves. How does loving your neighbor become a purer, more unencumbered act if you are freed from the clutches of the Love Idol?

2. What do you think it means to love *from* our approval, instead of *for* our approval?

3. Describe a specific time when you were able to love or serve someone else without any strings attached. How did that make you feel?

4. Name one specific action you could take this week to love or serve someone else, without expecting anything in return.

CHAPTER 13: APELLES

1. We have the means, through the Holy Spirit, to let people know that they are wildly adored and deeply cherished by the King. We are the changed ones, and the Love Idol has been smashed under our feet. How can we, the changed ones, now be the change agents? Where is God calling you to love people differently than the world does?

2. Once you're living in heaven, what do you most want to be remembered for on earth?

EPILOGUE

1. As you journey toward your forever home, how can you keep your eyes fixed on Jesus rather than on the sidelines at whoever might be watching? How does it change things today to know that Christ wants to give you the highest compliment of all: "Well done, my good and faithful servant"? (See Matthew 25:21.)

    Dear Lord, I believe by faith that there really is a finish line and that all of my striving will one day end. And I know that You are waiting there for me. May I always be content in knowing that You long to speak these words over me when I see You face-to-face: "Well done, my good and faithful servant." Thank You for loving me and for laying Your life down for me. Your fathomless love has the power to change the world, and it is already changing me. Until I see You at the finish line, help me run with perseverance the race marked out for me, fixing my eyes on You, the pioneer and perfecter of my faith. Amen.

Acknowledgments

How DOES ONE BEGIN to thank all the people who breathe hope and truth and wisdom into one book . . . and into one woman? It might seem like a book is a solo effort, but the act of putting words between covers isn't done in isolation. I will never be able to say thank you enough, but I've gotten a bit teary eyed while trying.

I am indebted to so many people, and to one great Savior, for a journey that became a book. To each of you, I offer my deepest thanks.

To Bill Jensen, for wise counsel and an uncompromising adherence to biblical truth.

To the entire Tyndale Momentum team, for believing in this project, for seeing the vision, for taking a chance on a farmwife and storyteller in Iowa, and for a tireless dedication to the gospel. Kim Miller, your sharp eyes, your prayers, and your Jesus-heart have made such a difference to the book, and to me. My thanks, also, to Jan Long Harris, Sarah Atkinson, Sharon Leavitt, Beth Sparkman,

Nancy Clausen, Yolanda Sidney, Brittany Buczynski, and Debbie Greer.

To the Our Savior's Lutheran Church community, for being a safe place under that steeple, right out here where the tall corn grows.

To those who shared stories: Shari, Trish, Jessica, Lorretta, Hazel, and others whose names didn't make it onto the pages but whose stories made it into the collective heart of this book. We are in this together, until that Great Day when we cross the finish line and our faith becomes sight.

To every blog reader and subscriber, for all you've done to encourage me and one another in the faith. You were the first to make me believe this was possible.

To the High Calling team and network, for the gift of genuine online community.

To Ann Kroeker, Laura Boggess, Deidra Riggs, Michelle DeRusha, Patty Horstman, Lyla Lindquist, Glenda VerMeer, and Susan Tjaden, for enthusiasm and encouragement very early on.

To Ann Voskamp, for reaching across a table at Laity Lodge on a Friday night and for believing in a book before I did. Thank you for continuing to reach across these one thousand miles that separate our farms. You are a generous friend.

To Lisa-Jo Baker, for standing so closely beside me as these words enter the world.

To Chris and Kathy Godfredsen, for the grace of your

friendship and for being the first to tell me that "the cure is the process."

To Ken Fuson, one of my all-time favorite newsmen, for reading the earliest draft. You knew you were holding my heart.

To Jenn Jenson, for your earnest prayers and steadfast friendship.

To Michelle Hage, for being Christ to me when I felt invisible, for loving me through all these years, and for "sharing a brain." I know Jesus better because I know you. You and Rob are a gift to me and Scott.

To our friends in Haiti, for living the truth about real love.

To my prayer team. You've spoken life into my hard days. And you've celebrated with me on the best days. You've been the truest friends and "fr-amily."

To this amazing family: Juliann, Mark, Lynda, Mike, John, Lisa, Mark, Becky, Aimee, Tye, Joyce, and all the kids, for cheering and praying.

To my parents, for letting me know that I never had to earn your love, and for loving me whether I was first or last.

To Lydia and Anna. You have made me a better me. Thank you for being the reason. I hope you never question how much your dad and I love you. And even more than that, I hope you always know how much you are already loved by Jesus.

To Scott, for always believing, even when I couldn't. For reading every page, and every draft, for tolerating too many frozen-pizza nights, and for talking me off a few cliffs. And mostly, for your enduring love. God's got it; yes, He does. And I'm so glad He's got us.

And to my Savior. I love to tell the story. Can it be my theme in glory? My heart broke wide open with this book. I prayed again and again that You would help me effectively communicate a message to people about how much they matter to You. And then, when I was tapping out those final words on a dark night with the moon rising outside the window, I felt it deeply: You were whispering the same thing to me. You were letting me know that I matter to You. And no matter how much our hearts break open, Yours broke even wider, to show us just how much You love us, and how that love can change the world.

About the Author

JENNIFER DUKES LEE used to cover crime, politics, and natural disasters as an award-winning news journalist. Now Jennifer uses her reporting skills to chase after the biggest scoop in history: the redemptive story of Christ. That's front-page news. She loves to tell the story; 'twill be her theme in glory!

Jennifer clings to the hope of the Cross, and she's passionate about sharing the Good News through story. She believes in miracles; she is one. She marvels at God's unrelenting grace for people who mess up—stumbling sinners like her, who have been made whole through Christ.

Jennifer is a storyteller and a grace dweller, and she invites you to join her on her blog at www.JenniferDukesLee.com and also at www.TheHighCalling.org, where she serves as a contributing editor.

She and her husband, Scott, met while attending Iowa State University in Ames. They returned to the Lee family's century-old farm near Inwood, Iowa, in 2002. They have two daughters, Lydia and Anna.

Jennifer invites you to connect with her on Twitter @dukeslee.

Online Discussion *guide*

TAKE *your* TYNDALE READING EXPERIENCE *to the* NEXT LEVEL

A FREE discussion guide for this book
is available at bookclubhub.net, perfect
for sparking conversations in your book
group or for digging deeper into the text
on your own.

www.bookclubhub.net

*You'll also find free discussion guides for
other Tyndale books, e-newsletters, e-mail
devotionals, virtual book tours, and more!*

Are your innermost thoughts robbing you of health and happiness?

Jennifer Crow tried to do everything right. So she was shocked when her seemingly perfect life began to fall apart. Diagnosed with a dozen chronic health issues, she entered a deep depression and spiritual crisis. And as everything unraveled, Jennifer began to see how the perfect lies she'd told herself—like the lies many of us believe—were literally crippling her body, mind, and soul.

In *Perfect Lies*, Jennifer reveals the nine key lies that held her back, walks us through her journey of miraculous recovery, and shares practical techniques for how we can overcome these same lies in our own lives and find true freedom.